THE PERSISTENCE OF MEMORY

NEW MEXICO'S CHURCHES

PHOTOGRAPHS BY ROBERT BREWER

TEXT BY STEVE MCDOWELL

FOREWORD BY ROBERT COLES

MUSEUM OF NEW MEXICO PRESS

SANTA FE

The Museum of New Mexico Press is a unit of the Museum of New Mexico, a division of the State Office of Cultural Affairs.

This publication was supported by a generous loan from the Office of Cultural Affairs' Revolving Fund.

Library of Congress Cataloging-in-Publication Data

Brewer, Robert, 1950–
    The persistence of memory: New Mexico's churches / photographs by Robert Brewer: text by Steve McDowell: foreword by Robert Coles.
        p.   cm.
    ISBN 0-89013-206-2.—ISBN 0-89013-207-0 (pbk.)
    1. Rio Grande Valley—Social life and customs.   2. Churches—Rio Grande Valley—History.   3. Rio Grande Valley—Church history.   4. Spaniards—Rio Grande Valley—History. 5. Churches—Rio Grande Valley—Pictorial works.   I. McDowell, Steve.   II. Title.
F802.R5B74   1990
978.9'02-dc20   90-30847
                                                          CIP

Project editor, Mary Wachs
Design by Jos. Trautwein
Printed in Singapore

Museum of New Mexico Press
P.O. Box 2087
Santa Fe, New Mexico 87504–2087

ACKNOWLEDGEMENTS

I was sitting at the art institute contemplating the future. Not the *big* future, but more along the lines of the coming summer — then only a couple weeks away. Out of the blue a great deal landed at my doorstep. I was given the invitation to go to a new place, this New Mexico place — both as a guest and to earn summer credit. As these six hours of summer credit parlayed into sixteen years, certain conclusions became inescapable. Large amounts of commitment and heavy doses of randomness even each other out. Singlemindedness and clarity work best in hindsight and are seldom a substitute for overkill. More importantly, patient support from loyal friends and family overcome a whole lot of the aforementioned pitfalls.

I would like to express appreciation and indebtedness to my wife, Becky, and kids, Robbie, Megan, and Abby, for believing that this undertaking had both a purpose and a conclusion. For the hours and weeks that sort of slipped away, thanks for your love and understanding. To Dick Rudisill, for your unfailing patience, guidance, and "nudges" that kept perspectives on track. Always your faith gave me confidence. Dad, as much as anything there is this overwhelming need for your approval. This project that seemed to drain resources endlessly but have no end: at long last we are there. And thanks to you, Mary, for taking this work off the streets. Thanks for taking risks.

Yet it would be totally self-indulgent to believe a story of this sort could be a one-way dialogue. The villagers, ranchers, *mayordomos*, and other New Mexicans that gave of themselves to two strangers provided the impetus to believe that this was something worth pursuing. Indeed, New Mexico, this is the book you gave to us.

Finally, there were the proofreaders, opinion givers, gate openers, and friends who helped us keep this all straight — more or less! Laurie, John, Gary and Marilyn, Danny and Yvonne, Gabrielle, Rudy, Gary, Carol and Joe, Lissa, Martha and Pat, Laura, Donna, Nancy, Bill and Barbara, José, Connie and Larry, Sandra, Eduardo, Dexter, Arthur, Tom, Charlie, Vic, Edith, Fathers John, Thomas, Austin, José, Roca, and Blanch; and finally, Archbishop Robert Sanchez.

Thanks also to the New Mexico Community Foundation for guidance, encouragement, and the privilege of slinging adobe on occasion.

BOB BREWER

First, the many *mayordomos* and community members who shared their time, churches, and memories with us; their warmth and hospitality and opening of doors have been the foundation of the whole project.

Dr. Richard Rudisill has been a guardian angel to the project, keeping the candle lit.

Laurel Seth and the good doctors John Kessell and Tom Holien amiably undertook the thankless task of proofreading; the book is more accurate and readable because of their efforts and suggestions.

Thanks again to you all.

STEVE MCDOWELL

For RITCHIE

When my wife, Jane, and I began our work in New Mexico—
talking with Pueblo Indian children and children whose ancestors came from Mexico, from Spain—we soon enough came to
appreciate the strong religious side in the lives of many families we were meeting. Not that families all over America don't
hold strong attachments to one or another church. But among
those we met north of Albuquerque and Santa Fe, the signifi-
cance of a Spanish Catholicism, as it has endured in the Southwest and responded to a Pueblo cultural tradition, became
vividly apparent at certain moments, especially when a grandmother or grandfather sat with us, even as we were sitting with
certain children, and shared thoughts and experiences—
moments in a long life nearing its end.

As I looked at the fine photographs in this book—so evoca-
tive of a whole world, its stillness, its solitude, its strength and
dignity—and as I read the suggestive, even lyrical text, so well
suited in tone to the photographs and subject matter both, I
thought of some of the New Mexico churches my wife, sons, and
I attended during our years there—and the people we knew

who came regularly, and were not reluctant, as we became friends, to talk about a certain "persistence of memory" in their own lives. Carla, for instance—a lady of eighty-one, straight-backed, tall, still with a few strands of black hair amid the white, and most noticeable of all, wide eyes that miss very little. "When I remember myself as a little girl," she once said, "I think of my grandfather, holding my hand." She told us more, of course: "He was stooped. I try to hold myself up, so I won't get that way. He warned me: 'Don't let yourself get bent over—your eyes will always be looking down, down, at the ground, and our sky will be beyond you.' I can see him, right now, stretching himself, working so hard with every muscle in his body to look at our sky—it brought peace to him; it brings peace to me and my family. I can see him—as if it was only today we were together—walking toward our church, my little hand in his big one. He'd work so hard to lift his head, his eyes toward the church, then the cross on top, and then the sky, where we both knew Jesus must be smiling and thanking us for remembering Him. For me, my grandfather's right hand—all those years of work.—were a part of being in church. He'd hold my hand while we sat and prayed. That hand seemed as big as our sky! When the priest asked us to pray, I pictured Jesus and my grandfather smiling and talking, and I knew I was lucky, to be there in that church, with both of them. All these years I still remember those times—I can close my eyes and see the church, so plain and simple. My son drove me down to Albuquerque once, and took me to a big church there. I felt lost. I wondered how our Lord feels! He liked to be with a small group of people—and now, these big places, filled with more families than I ever knew existed.

"When I was sick once my grandfather got my mother [his daughter] very upset. He got me out of bed and I got dressed, and he carried me all the way to church. He was going to take me on his horse, but he worried the trip would be shaky. I can remember him right now—walking with me in his arms. He sang. He said a prayer. He told me stories. He made me laugh. When we got to the church, he took me toward the altar. He sat down with me on his lap in the front row. He said a prayer, and he pointed to me while he prayed. I realized he was crying. I was upset, but then he smiled, and I could see that he was happy. He trusted Jesus; I know that today. Oh, I think I knew it back then, too. He believed that Jesus was the greatest of doctors—and He is! He believed that Jesus lived in that church; that's what he always told me: let us go and have a talk with Jesus; He is there, in the shadows of the church, and He will pay attention, and He will not forget you!' To this day, I see my grandfather in that church, and Jesus sitting beside him—the two smiling and good friends. I will be leaving soon, and I

hope I will be joining them. I hope the Lord decides I am worthy of my grandfather, and Jesus. I pray so in their church, each week I do."

So it goes, so it has gone, and I rather suspect—I hope and pray, too—so it will go at least for some in a land still full of "enchantment," no matter the dreary intrusion, these days, of slogans, plastic, fads, a huckster economy. A church for the old woman Clara was a place of devotion; a place where the mind's moral and spiritual imagination could be nourished, prompted to grow and exert its influence on a life; a place where neighbors and kin somehow come together, no matter the doubts and suspicions, the grudges and worse—an aspect of all our humanity. Most of all, as this book so wonderfully, tellingly informs us—those churches are repositories of what is sacred in the religious sense, yes, but also what is sacred about each and every one of us: the holy memories of our lives as they are handed from person to person, and thereby given what persistence each and all of us can manage.

ROBERT COLES

To carry a river-rounded stone for a day and feel a vague obligation toward it, to pick up an old tool whose handle has the warmth of an affable hand, or to stand in an ancient building and sense the lingering voices of a distant past is to know both the nuances of time and the limitations of language.

The vocabulary of time ranges in scale from the minuteness of nanoseconds to the vastness of the *kalpa*, a Hindu time span of more than four billion years. It is largely a language of durations, an array of measurements. When the strands of time and personal experience are woven tightly together, though, subtle and intricate patterns emerge that are beyond the reach of measured terms. Their complex textures and colors, difficult to describe, have tended to outrun the pursuits of language; many have remained nameless.

This brings an interesting paradox into view. Modern societies, some of the most time-obsessed that have ever existed, have either lost or overlooked the language for unobtrusive yet important manifestations of time—manifestations that have given the lives of individuals and cultures richer meaning since time beyond memory.

There are places and experiences that await this language, that will need it if their most essential qualities are to be retrieved from silence and anonymity. Among them are the hundreds of churches, built of aging adobe and stone, that are scattered across the high mesas and sandy valleys of the American Southwest.

19

Societies in the midst of dramatic transition, especially those that have turned their efforts toward novelty and mass production—whose arts and artifacts are designed to be obsolete, worn out, or simply abandoned before long—are a difficult place to find concepts for the beneficial blending of time and regard. It makes sense to search instead in slowly evolving, traditional cultures that celebrate endurance and continuity rather than change.

In the deserts of North Africa, where history is long and resources are short, the Moors use the term *baraka* to describe a special character in places or things. Many centuries ago, the word alluded to a quality imparted abruptly and dramatically—lightning bolts were among its most powerful causes. Through time, however, the force known as baraka was seen to be even stronger after its object enjoyed long use and appreciation. Gradually, it came to be regarded as a trait (almost a personality) that accumulates very slowly, culminating eventually in a sort of spirituality that has been described as *blessedness*.

Baraka might be imparted to almost any object, it is said, regardless of size or origin, but it seems to be found most often in things handmade or much-handled and is especially apt to appear in works of craftsmanship, artisanship, and folk art—precisely those objects, in other words, in which time, care, and affection have been mingled in the making.

These were the conditions, interwoven with history and terrain, that produced and preserved the adobe churches of the American Southwest. Important for many reasons—religious, historical, and architectural—the churches are also sought out for the difficult-to-describe quality of baraka they embody. It is one of history's nice ironies that the Moors, whose cultural and religious domination Spain suffered for more than seven centuries, might now offer the most sympathetic concept available for the Hispanic churches of the Rio Grande, yet so it seems.

Architecture is a form of memory, less similar to the structured mechanism of history than it is to a life-form, with a growth, adaptation, and life span that resemble those of an ancient tree. Among the most ancient of architectural materials, adobe provides a natural habitat for the deep-rooted memory known as baraka. Its sun-dried bricks are a confluence of time, hand labor, and chosen earth; the architecture they form is uniquely congenial toward the shaping influences of both nature and history.

In a sense, a truly new adobe structure cannot be built on the oldest sites. Adobe bricks made on long-used ground will be a reformation of the crushed and fallen bricks that preceded them there, bricks that were themselves a re-creation from their predecessors. The result, no matter how simple in form, will be complex—a synthesis of the present with the shards, ashes, and other traces left by life in the past.

Moving into what is now New Mexico, sixteenth-century Spanish colonists and missionaries settled among the long-established, strongly traditional people of the Pueblo tribes—a people guided by a concept of sacredness through time and use—*xayeh*—that was very close to what the Spaniards knew as baraka. The colonists, as they built on the ruins and amidst the centuries-old adobe villages they found in the Pueblo culture, followed the example not only of their compatriots at Mexico City but of a long-standing precedent throughout history, incorporating the old in the new, deepening the textures of time and experience.

The Spaniards' missions faithfully carried the pattern forward. They emerged as a new and unique architectural form, but a form whose constituent elements were old and well tried: native materials, the Pueblo style, the Franciscans' cruciform plan, and untold hours of intensive hand labor. The result was an architecture that, though it required constant care and attention, made a strong affirmative statement that it was meant to endure.

The era of the adobe church builders now appears nearly complete. In simple terms of scale, its churches became more and more modest over time. Yet certain traits in the work of its builders not only persist, as intended, but have continued to increase in effect and importance. Built on religious convictions, the churches preserve the elusive baraka often endangered in contemporary life.

Some believe that baraka, once evident, persists and never ebbs away; others feel that it needs to be nurtured by contact and renewed. The question is probably an old one, rather personal, and unlikely to be resolved in any final way—the sort of question that might occur to someone walking through the ruins of an adobe church.

When a pale, horizontal band begins to mark the mountains with a wide contour line a few thousand feet above the Rio Grande, the aspen have begun to turn and autumn has arrived in the Southwest. Seen by late twilight or in the early dawn, the faded leaves of the aspen might almost be the ghost of an intertidal shore, where the vast warm inland seas of the geologic past brushed up against their coast.

The ancient seas have, in fact, left their mark here; the painted deserts are marine silts, the mountains are home to fossil fish as well as trout, and the valleys are strewn in many places with smooth-tumbled stones and cobbles that the powerful tides and high-energy rivers of the geologic past have left behind. Over much of the Southwest, damp, low ground is caked with what once was sea salt.

The least breeze heard flowing through the restless leaves of an aspen grove can sound like the rush of a tide. But the aspen line the shores of an ocean of space, not sea. They have found a narrow niche to colonize, above the droughts but below the longest-lasting snow. Following the grasses out onto fire-opened meadows, they shelter the seedlings of the firs and other conifers that will eventually replace them, closing the meadows.

An aspen sheared of leaves can renew its foliage repeatedly in a single season, a rare resilience. Yet aspen, science now believes, have little of their energy invested in the life of an individual tree. The aspen of a whole hillside, of an entire grove, have proved to be part of an extended unity—interrelated and interconnected throughout their network of roots, each subtly aware of the circumstances of the others.

Graceful, tenacious, the aspen have so far resisted the best efforts of government and industry to turn them to profit, to bring them into the mainstream economy. Their principal value is to themselves, and to those who appreciate them for what they are and for the unique experience it is to wander among them.

Explorers, hunters, and refugees have been traveling the lands now known as the American Southwest for more than ten thousand years. The earliest are shadowy figures, still little known to science. Wandering in small groups, they left as traces a scattering of well-worked spear points and some circles of fire-cracked stones, but no sign of the impressions the landscape of their time might have made at first acquaintance.

Subtle clues, such as pollen buried deep in the dust of caves, suggest that a traveler in the Southwest ten millennia ago would have found a land of rich savannas and shallow lakes, left mild and abundant by a waning Ice Age. A long, steady trend toward warmer and drier conditions followed, dramatically interrupted by lava flows and clouds of ash when dormant volcanic forces reawoke from time to time. During the past several thousand years, however, anyone entering the region has encountered a semi-arid terrain rather similar to that of our own time.

The recent era, marked off in nature by a dry climate, has a strong and recurrent pattern among its human settlers as well: cultures arrive, consolidate themselves, flourish, and then—somewhat mysteriously at this point—vanish. The Hohokam, the Mimbres, and the city builders of Chaco and of Mesa Verde each apparently chose to walk away from what we now consider their greatest accomplishments. The causes of these abandonments were probably complex: disease, warfare, and environmental abuse may all have come into play. Some groups were apparently absorbed by stronger or more successful tribes, gradually disappearing into a fabric of cultural blending. As important as these factors are, however, there is another element even more essential for the peoples of the Southwest: drought has always been a key player in the drama of the region (and may well be again), and there are cultures in its long, unwritten past that might be said, in effect, to have evaporated.

Sixteenth-century Spaniards, entering for the first time a territory that they called *Nuevo Méjico*, encountered a landscape still relatively unaffected by man. They found its forests, wildlife, and tall-grass tablelands in a nearly pristine state of abundance. Yet one central and irreducible fact asserted itself to them as it had asserted itself to all life in the semi-arid and desert terrain of the recent Southwest: water is survival.

Don Juan de Oñate and several hundred would-be colonists, accompanied by a contingent of Franciscan missionaries, started north toward New Mexico from a small village called Santa Barbara in 1598. Traveling on foot, on horseback, or in crude carts, their entire journey would be set in severe desert terrain where prickly pear, creosote bush, and ocotillo cactus were the dominant figures on a background of rocks and sand.

The desert didn't tempt the colonists to linger. Moving as quickly as possible, they pushed northward until reaching a defensible place whose lands could support agriculture. Their expectations included hopes for gold or silver, but they knew they wouldn't be likely to repeat the exploits of Pizarro in Peru or those of Cortés in Mexico. Northward-searching journeys by Coronado in 1540 and others in the fifty years following had found no rich indigenous nations to conquer and no other obvious or easy sources of wealth. The upper Rio Grande and its tributaries were home to a centuries-old culture, but the limits imposed on its people by a harsh terrain left little room for splendor. A settlement established among them would serve primarily as a base for further exploration of a vast new region.

Oñate and his straggling column traveled an open, shadeless country where heat and dehydration were constant, but where it was possible to cover great distances each day. Good and sufficient water (for thousands of cattle, sheep, and goats, in addition to the colonists and their horses) was scarce over most of the route they chose, part of which eventually became known as the *Jornada del Muerto*—Journeyplace of the Deadman. Where their route lay nearer the water, woods, and thickets of the Rio Grande, they must have been tempted to stop in the river's lower valley, yet there were no permanent Indian settlements there—for good reason. The Pueblos had long known the dangers of the lower river: its moods of drought and flood were extreme, while the desert at the edge of its floodplain was a treeless dominion of heat and thirst.

The colonists finally settled on the confluence of the Rio Grande and one of its largest tributaries, the red and silt-laden Rio Chama. The two rivers meet in a delta of damp ground, bounded and shaded by a deep stand of cottonwoods at the water's edge—an irresistible refuge for anyone who had just crossed the Chihuahuan desert at the height of summer heat, in the company of seven thousand head of livestock and the languid dust cloud they undoubtedly carried along.

The site selected by Oñate was a natural choice, and one that had been made before. Ancestors of the people of San Juan Pueblo had settled at the confluence centuries earlier. For Oñate, this meant that his colonists could move into massive, multistoried adobe buildings in the traditional Pueblo architectural style. For the residents of San Juan, unfortunately, it meant that hundreds of armed strangers were moving on their homes.

Taking shelter at San Juan solved the colonists' most immediate problem, so Oñate turned to other concerns. He soon showed the priorities he saw dictated by the unfamiliar landscape that surrounded him: as fortifications were unnecessary, he instead started work in late summer on the first church in the Southwest—but only after setting up, several weeks earlier, a system of irrigation ditches to help protect his colony from the arid climate.

The first mass in Oñate's new church took place during San Juan's vibrant autumn, and a day later members of the colony celebrated by presenting the first play written and produced north of the Rio Grande. Yet celebration couldn't have been the only note evoked by the season; Oñate must have been troubled by the sparse harvest the Pueblo farmers brought in, especially as snow often returns to the high crests of the nearby Sangre de Cristo mountains in September, a dramatic omen of the oncoming winter.

The winter of 1598 was, indeed, to be a harsh test for the colony. Some of the Pueblos in the region risked a fierce revolt, killing several of Oñate's soldiers. A disillusioned faction among the colony's troops mutinied. Even more serious was the shortage of food: the native people at San Juan, though still outwardly friendly, simply did not have enough to support the Spaniards until the following spring. Even after the colonists had seized much of the pueblo's harvest (over strong objections from the Franciscans), they were eventually forced to gamble on the edibility of unfamiliar wild plants.

The events of 1599 began to evoke some disquieting patterns for the Spaniards; back, for example, were brilliant skies that stayed open for weeks on end, with drought seeming to crouch constantly just over the horizon, ready to pounce on the fields. When rain did fall, it was often from immense thunderheads in violent storms worth little to crops. In spite of the lesson of the previous winter, there were colonists who still hoped for some kind of a bonanza, rejecting the thought of farming for a living and refusing to work in the fields.

Oñate himself spent increasing time and energy searching for something more lucrative than parched subsistence crops. In June of 1601, he left San Juan to pursue new rumors of a fabled city in more benign country. Virtually his entire colony—settlers, troops, and nearly all of the missionaries—deserted while he was gone. Convinced that their governor's efforts were futile, they had fled toward Mexico with everything they could carry. Oñate barely managed to

gather just enough of the deserters, along with new colonists and missionaries, to return to San Juan and revive the flagging colony.

A last, desperate foray led Oñate and a detachment of troops to the mouth of the Colorado River in 1605. It was essentially a prospecting party, lured westward by the chance of a mineral strike, then carried on to the Gulf of California by the possibility of pearls and a route to the China trade. Like all previous attempts, it only deepened doubts about the value of the new lands.

In 1607, Oñate decided to concede the struggle and resign as governor. By 1614 he had been charged, arrested, and fined by the officers of the Crown in Mexico City. Although a number of charges were laid against him, in essence Don Juan de Oñate was convicted of failure to form a rich Spanish outlier in the lands of Nuevo Méjico, from whence he was banished forever.

Oñate's storm-ridden tenure as governor was productive perhaps in one sense: it revealed most of the elements that would dominate New Mexico's history for the next two hundred years. Early Spanish hopes for the region had been based on gold and the discovery of legendary kingdoms; the reality consisted of a large number of reluctant, sometimes hostile converts to Christianity and an uncertain harvest of beans, corn, and squash. Yet the Spanish in the Southwest had already begun to prove that their central trait was tenacity, not optimism. They intended, at all costs, to stay.

New Mexico at the time of Oñate's departure had begun to look like a rather barren prospect to civil authorities in Mexico City. But the Franciscan Order had a different vision of the northern frontier; they saw thousands of pagan souls that might be brought into the fold of Christianity and European culture. Franciscan missionaries moved slowly but steadily north to the new province, and their influence from the beginning was far out of proportion to their numbers.

Both civil and religious leaders in New Mexico had realized early that, for the time being at least, the native people of the Southwest were its only evident resource. The Indians became the focus of a fierce church/state conflict with grave consequences for all concerned, involving even that most formidable of seventeenth-century institutions, the Holy Office of the Inquisition.

The outlines of the conflict were simple: the governors and leading citizens of the territory saw the Indians as an extensive supply of cheap labor and a source of tributes, while the missionaries tended to view them as an extensive supply of cheap labor and a source of considerable religious energy. Each side, naturally, assumed that its own authority over the Indians was absolute.

The Franciscans were few in number, but they had many advantages in their contest with civil adversaries. Close-knit and well organized, they had fairly clear goals and were prepared to undergo great austerities, self-sacrifice, and even martyrdom. Their efforts in New Mexico had been remarkable from the start. Many thousands of the native people had been converted, nominally at least, with conversions followed by instruction in music and languages (Latin and Spanish), the liturgy, and in improved techniques of agriculture and construction. These efforts didn't go unnoticed by the Spanish Crown; they redesignated New Mexico (previously a proprietary colony in private hands) as a royal colony, largely on the strength of reports that emphasized both Oñate's failures and the friars' successes.

The Franciscans worked diligently to replace the curves and arcs of Pueblo kivas, most of which were embedded in earth or stone, with the high-rising towers and cruciform plans of mission churches. Between forty-five and fifty churches had been built by 1660, the work of scarcely a hundred friars and their legion of converts. Time spent shaping native materials seemed to echo the missionaries' view of what they sought to accomplish. Using the adobe, sandstone, and rough-hewn beams that had characterized southwestern architecture throughout its centuries of prehistory, they joined the ranks of the most industrious builders in the region, raising structures as ambitious as the Great Kivas of Chaco Canyon and the cliff cities of Mesa Verde. By comparison, New Mexico's territorial governors and private citizenry managed in their first hundred years to found one new town (their capital at Santa Fe) and a handful of smaller settlements, while abandoning Oñate's riverside settlement beside the people of San Juan Pueblo.

The seventeenth-century missions were massive structures up to a hundred and fifty feet in length, with walls up to ten feet thick and clerestoried ceilings that rose to thirty feet or more. Integrating native materials and styles with conventional European religious plans, they were a new and distinct architectural form. In many pueblos, the new churches tended to dominate the low, flat-roofed architecture around them, and although the Franciscans' religious and cultural domination was not as dramatic, it too was formidable and growing.

Yet governors, citizens, and soldiers had their designs on the future as well, and strife over power-sharing between the priests and civil authorities became an unrelenting constant. Governors were rebuked and banished; priests were recalled. The infrequent southbound mails became loaded with complaints, countercharges, and appeals for the authorities in Mexico City, and ultimately in Spain, to contend with.

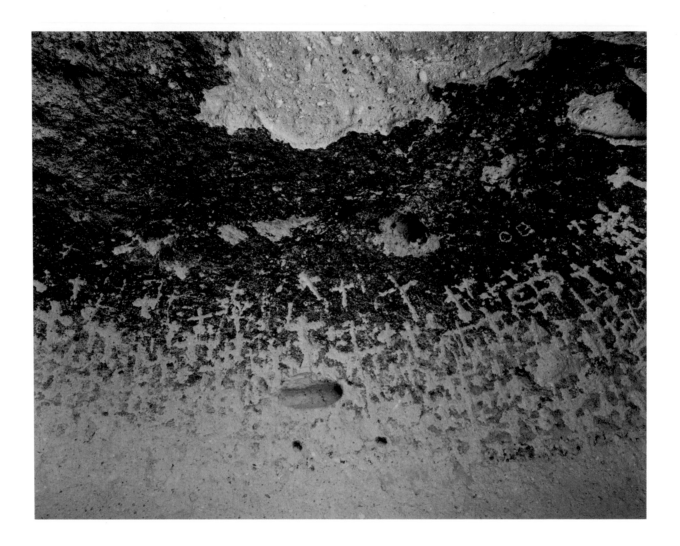

Priests and politicians alike were frequently reminded that natural forces—droughts, floods, and frost—might have the last word on their fates in New Mexico. Instead, it proved to be the Indians that made the most forceful statement of the seventeenth century.

Apache and Navajo raiders emerged from lands far beyond the horizons of the Rio Grande settlements, lands still little-known to the Spanish. In ever greater numbers, they poured through mountain passes and down into the valleys to plunder storehouses, seize horses and weapons, and carry away captives. As any season of food shortages intensified, so did the incursions of raiders. Attacks became so severe and frequent in the 1670s that several Pueblo villages at the edge of the plains were abandoned and with them their missions, including those whose brooding ruins can still be seen at Quarai, Abo, and Gran Quivira.

The Pueblos suffered heavy losses from all quarters. In Oñate's time they are believed to have numbered at least sixty thousand persons, occupying one hundred and thirty traditional stone-and-adobe towns. By 1679, after the combined effects of European diseases, armed conflict, and forced tribute of their crops, fewer than half that number (possibly as few as ten thousand) still survived; eighty pueblos had been abandoned. It may have seemed imminent that the Pueblo culture would ebb away into history, but the time came when the Pueblos who remained, their culture suppressed and their labors seldom for their own, would tolerate no more.

In 1680, the Pueblos united to drive the Spanish off their homelands. They killed most of the priests within reach, then laid siege to Santa Fe (still the only Spanish town in New Mexico). As they began to burn outlying ranches (the *estancias*), the Spanish colonists realized that they had no choice but to retreat hundreds of miles to the south. Most of the mission churches were heavily damaged or destroyed, their altars, santos, and other symbols broken or burned. In a matter of days, the work of the seventeenth-century friar-architects was nearly swept away.

The great storm of events in 1680, usually called the Pueblo Revolt, was just the beginning of a Pueblo-Spanish war lasting over fifteen years. The revenge-forged alliance between Pueblo warriors and those of other tribes drove the Spaniards completely off the Pueblo homelands in 1680, but it was a strike that did not hold; nearly as soon as the Spanish were gone, the alliance began to break down. For over a decade Spanish settlers stayed far to the south, and a half-hearted attempt at reconquest was turned back in 1692. But by 1695 there was again a Spanish official, Don Diego de Vargas, ruling New Mexico from the Palace of the Governors at Santa Fe, and the Franciscans had returned with him.

In June of 1696, a number of Pueblos joined together to resist the reoccupation, killing five priests and twenty-one of de Vargas's colonists. But this time the fires did not spread. The 1680 alliance of Pueblos and other warriors wasn't repeated, and Spanish troops prevailed easily in a series of small, isolated skirmishes. By the end of 1696, the Spanish reconquest of New Mexico was essentially complete.

Confident of the new peace along the Rio Grande, the Spanish now ventured out to found new settlements on the river and its tributaries. The towns of Santa Cruz, Bernalillo, and Albuquerque had all appeared on the map by 1716, each with a new church begun as soon as its townsite was established. The austerities of the land and the climate were, in one small respect at least, an advantage for these new settlers and church-building friars: desert sand and clay (almost free of organic material) combine with long periods of sun and dry heat as the perfect conditions for the formation of adobe bricks.

Minor amenities were increasing. Wheat, chile, apples, and onions, crops introduced by way of a yearlong cart journey from Mexico, enhanced the nutrition of the frontier diet and helped ease its daunting monotony.

Wagon caravans, arriving as seldom as once in every three years, were new Mexico's lifeline. They brought mail, news, and trade goods, though in fact New Mexico had precious little to trade away. There were sheep and cattle raised on the territory's seemingly limitless grasslands; the tanned hides of cattle, buffalo, and deer; woolen blankets that the Pueblos were forced to weave; and non-Pueblo Indian captives—taken altogether, not nearly enough to cover the many essentials the colonists had to import. For the rest, the colony relied on direct official support from Mexico City, where authorities at times must have regarded their Apache-haunted supply trains as a dubious investment, a combination of charity and the burdensome support of their vaguely defined territorial claims in the far north.

The Franciscans faced an equally stark situation. Setting out to reestablish their missions as soon as the reconquest was complete, they found many adobe and stone walls still sound but only the great mission of San Esteban de Acoma relatively intact in structure. Nor did the ruins of the pre-Revolt churches hold much worth salvaging. Almost all of their furnishings had been destroyed or had disappeared; even the clappers of the bells were gone.

Gone as well was much of the friars' crucial support from Mexico, while old rifts with civil authorities in the colony reopened. The pre-Revolt missions were gradually rebuilt, though often on a smaller scale than before, and the process of converting the Indians began again. At the same time a steadily growing population of new settlers (who soon outnumbered the Pueblos) called for more time and resources. Still, it seemed that the hopes of the Franciscans for the new province had been scaled down even more than their churches and convents.

Spanish interest in the Southwest broadened geographically during the eighteenth century, embracing not only Texas and the Gulf coast, but Sonora and southern Arizona. Members of the Pima, Papago, Yaqui, and various other tribes of the Sonoran deserts were served by the Jesuits, most notably Eusebio Kino. Starting in 1687, Kino founded twenty-five missions among the Pimas before his death in 1711, all built in the style of their counterparts further south in Mexico. In addition, a rich silver strike made in 1736 (at the namesake town of Arizona, just a few miles south of the present Mexico-Arizona line) gave northern Sonora and southern Arizona a viability that Spanish New Mexico never attained.

New Mexico's eighteenth-century Spanish settlers gradually moved beyond the major river valleys of the Rio Grande, the Chama, and the Pecos to found small villages and *ranchos* as far from the protection of troops as they dared. Attacks by Apache, Navajo, and Comanche continued. The Franciscans, whose work had once been centered in their Pueblo missions, now found their dwindling resources spread ever thinner by a burgeoning, dispersing Spanish population and by the rigors of travel over arduous terrain.

The justly famous churches of Las Trampas and Ranchos de Taos, completed between 1760 and 1815, were the last large-scale buildings attempted by the missionaries, exceptions in a trend toward smaller and plainer structures. Throughout the eighteenth century, the initiative in church construction shifted steadily toward private citizens and occasionally to civil authorities. The architectural style evolved by the pre-Revolt friars remained strong, but in other respects the Franciscans' influence continued to wane.

Settlers were moving out toward any valley or mesa with adequate water, grazing, and possible cropland. They often went geographically and financially beyond the ability of the Franciscans to provide for their religious needs. An adaptation inevitably arose to deal with these needs in the emergence of one of the most distinctive elements of Hispanic culture in the Southwest, the *Cofradía de Nuestra Padre Jesus Nazareno*—the religious society of laymen known today as the Penitente Brotherhood.

Religious societies whose rites center on atonement and penitence existed long before the Spanish arrived in the New World; a tradition of religious self-punishment goes back at least to thirteenth-century Europe. Yet conditions of life on the New Mexican frontier, where death and deprivation were a constant presence, seem especially conducive to it.

The Penitente Order in New Mexico originated as a response to the shortage of priests in the territory and was encouraged and guided by the Franciscans initially when it first appeared in the eighteenth century. Later, both the friars and other church officials tried to discourage what they viewed as a form of extremism, but the Brotherhood continued to grow long after it had come completely under the control of laymen.

The Penitentes' customs reflected conditions of life in villages and on ranches far from town life, where a conservative, self-sufficient people were long-accustomed to austerity. Their chapels, known as *moradas*, were plain, single-storied buildings often consisting of a single room where the culmination of the religious calendar was—and is—the reenactment of the Passion during *Semana Santa*, or Holy Week.

Much has been made of crucifixions, cactus whips, and blood in Penitente ceremonialism. Lurid accounts and the trampling of curiosity seekers have added secretiveness and heavily draped windows to the Penitentes' other traits. Little notice has been taken of their benevolent activities. As the secular and religious worlds have continued to change around them, Penitente tradition has remained nearly intact, a monument to the character of religous life in the past as enduring as the stone and adobe missions.

Eighteenth-century New Mexico, after the sound and fury of the previous hundred years, must have seemed becalmed. Internally static, it was almost suspended from the flow of outside events by its isolation. Trade into the territory had begun to pass through Chihuahua, much nearer than Mexico City, but the shift made little material difference. In 1776, Fray Francisco Atanasio Dominguez made a church-ordered inspection of the missions of New Mexico. His detailed report, though it praised some churches and churchmen, described a system in decline. Raids by non-Pueblo Indians, church/state antagonism, drought, and disease epidemics had become routine. As the nineteenth century opened, however, there were signs of change.

Few foreigners had made their way into New Mexico during the eighteenth century; those few were either traders or trappers tempted to southwestern streams by beaver and the soaring prices in the international fur market. Such forays were illegal under Spanish law, but they were of minor concern to the Spaniards—unlike the round of international intrigues and transactions that followed.

The immense and vaguely defined area known as the Louisiana Territory was ceded by Spain to the French in 1800; just three years later, France in turn sold it to the United States, where some took the view that these new holdings reached to the Rio Grande. This was ominous for the Spanish, whose lands in what is now Texas had already been invaded in 1801 by Americans.

Concern mounted further with the appearance in New Mexico of Zebulon Pike, an American military man the Spanish correctly suspected of being a spy. In 1813 there was a revolution in Texas, carried out with American backing, that established a Republic of Texas lasting four months. Spanish authority on their northeastern frontier was crumbling rapidly. In 1821, leaders far south of Santa Fe declared independence from Spain. The colony on the upper Rio Grande was suddenly part of the new nation of Mexico.

Mexican independence did not, of course, bring Santa Fe and Mexico City any closer together by way of the long, arduous road that connected them overland. It did, however, affect the political and economic distances—adversely, as the two places were even farther apart under Mexican flags than before. A rapidly changing series of governments in turmoil at Mexico City had little time or money for the poor and dependent northern territory, which was left to fare for itself. The Santa Fe trade had been forced to flow through Mexico in the past, but no longer; commerce with the Americans to the east soon developed. In 1824, a party of Santa Feans traveled to the Mississippi River to invite trade and propose a trail, but the talk was scarcely needed. The Santa Fe trail, in effect, established itself, its supplies moving toward strong demand. American freight wagons began to pour into the Mexican territory, and, along with their goods, they brought the influences of the United States steadily nearer New Mexico.

New Mexico in 1821 was home to roughly forty thousand souls, and the number was rising. This population was under the care of no more than twenty-odd friars and a handful of the secular priests who were intended, eventually, to replace the Franciscans throughout the territory. Already hard-pressed by their small numbers and the vastness of their area of responsibility, the priests met another setback when compulsory tithing was outlawed by the Mexican congress in 1833. This law lifted a considerable burden from the general population, but it made priests and churches directly dependent on the meager resources of

their parishioners. Priests, their numbers dwindling, now became itinerant; each served as wide an area as he was able. The churches entered a period of decline and abandonment. By the middle of the 1840s, only one Franciscan friar still served in all of New Mexico.

The power of the Mexican territorial government had eroded virtually from its inception in 1821 and was barely able to contain an uprising among dissatisfied citizens and Pueblo sympathizers in 1837. Government troops had little trouble stopping the column of Texans that made a half-hearted attempt (not soon forgotten) to capture New Mexico in 1841, but in August of 1846 Stephen Watts Kearny marched a detachment of troops into Santa Fe and declared the authority of the United States over New Mexico. The territory's Mexican period came to an end with some muttered curses and a few tears, but with no shots fired.

Transition from Spanish to Mexican authority had scarcely affected the structure of civil, military, or religious institutions in New Mexico. American control of the Southwest brought rapid and dramatic changes, and even the most isolated villagers scattered over the upper Rio Grande soon found these changes coming to their church.

A new diocese was created at Santa Fe in 1850, with the French-born Jean Baptiste Lamy as its first bishop. Bishop Lamy took charge of the Catholic church over an area of nearly a quarter of a million square miles, an area whose closest bishop in the preceding three centuries had been at Durango, Mexico, nearly a thousand miles to the south.

The energy and enthusiasm characteristic of the seventeenth-century friars returned to the Rio Grande in the personality of Bishop Lamy. At the time of his arrival, New Mexico had a population of some sixty-five thousand persons served by a total of nine secular priests. Lamy soon had forty priests in the field, while construction of new churches and restoration of neglected ones were begun. He traveled thousands of miles throughout the Southwest, avid for first-hand experience of the vast, complex territory now under his authority.

Lamy's character and sense of mission allowed little room for compromise, and he was not without his adversaries. The state of the church when he first arrived had shocked him, and some have seen cultural chauvinism in his approach to reform. Perhaps symbolically, Lamy imported Italian stonemasons to replace the old adobe church he inherited at Santa Fe with a cathedral of dressed stone built in orthodox European style. He looked to France rather than to Spain or Mexico for his new priests and nuns, and worked to have the Penitente Brotherhood disbanded. He also felt that traditional religious practices

in the Pueblos had been given too much latitude and tried to suppress some aspects of their public ceremonies.

The new bishop may have seemed unsympathetic to the cultural differences in New Mexico, but there was little question of his dedication to better conditions in the still-frontierlike territory. Lamy established the first hospital and the first orphanage in the Southwest, as well as a college at Santa Fe. Made an archbishop in 1875, he became one of the territory's strongest advocates of public education, playing a leading role in efforts to establish a free public school system in New Mexico. The cathedral aside, the eighty-five new churches erected during his first fifteen years in New Mexico were nearly all adobe. Lamy and his new priests also moved to save many of the older adobe churches.

Lamy's French heritage was a dominant facet of his character, but in one respect he was a quintessentially Yankee leader: the past, with its grueling poverty and widespread suffering for the common people, held little charm for him. It is an apt metaphor for his outlook that he worked so persistently to replace New Mexico's rambling wagon trails with the steel tracks of the railroads. Rails did in fact reach the territory in 1879, and the mainline station closest to Lamy's new cathedral still bears his name.

The American presence was soon felt virtually everywhere in New Mexico. The suppression of Navajo and Apache raiding, for example, meant that villages, ranches, and farms could be established in places that had been too dangerous to settle for centuries. The railroad made goods and markets available to a territory once virtually stranded by the old ox-cart and wagon trade with Mexico and still hobbled economically by isolation even after the Santa Fe Trail came into play. Outgoing timber, sheep, and cattle became profitable on a large scale for the first time. Significant gold, silver, and copper strikes added intensity to an atmosphere that in some places began to look like a boom.

New Mexico's transition toward the American system was naturally not without problems, and one of the thorniest, still problematic in the twentieth century, was the handling of land grants made by the Spanish Crown. Formal American affirmation of these major landholdings had been part of the Treaty of Guadalupe Hidalgo of 1848, but this affirmation fell far short of guaranteeing grant lands against the steady pressure and sometimes sharp practice of lawyers, land speculators, tax collectors, and eager west-moving settlers. Conflicting water claims also became tangled, over time, into a knot nearly as tight as that formed by land-grant claims.

Land and water controversies were signs of a new and growing recognition that New Mexico's natural resources, and those of the West as a whole, were not inexhaustible. The region's long-standing competition for well-watered land broadened quickly in the 1860s and 1870s to embrace rangeland, timber, and potential mineral locations. Cattlemen who foresaw the end of the open range began to consolidate large deeded holdings and enclose them with barbed wire, bringing on a new class of conflict—the range war. At the same time, mining claims and timber tracts were being staked out in the remotest areas. Faced with runaway exploitation of public lands, an alarmed Congress in the 1880s moved to withdraw huge tracts across the West as preserves, de facto recognition that the frontier was gone.

Architecture is remarkably responsive to cultural change, and New Mexico's churches, residences, and commercial buildings reflected the influence of eastern styles and materials soon after U.S. annexation of the western territory. Fired brick quickly became the standard for military and commercial buildings. While most churches and homes built between 1846 and 1900 were still built of the traditional adobe, flat roofs covered with dirt and the once-ubiquitous oiled adobe floors began giving way to pitched tin roofs and milled flooring.

Some changes in the early part of the American period seem to invite an interpretation through metaphor, but with mixed results. Among the innovations railroaded into the Southwest were large paned windows, which allowed more light in New Mexico's churches than ever before. At the same time, the new pitched roofs caused lateral stresses that were too much for old adobe walls to stand, and many a venerable wall went down under the strain of the new "improvements." Milled lumber brought in for window frames, door frames, and doors made it easier for New Mexicans to carry on with their tradition of painting house openings in blue, the color of the Virgin of Guadalupe's cloak, to protect a household from both earthly and unearthly evils.

Taken as a whole, the nineteenth century brough increasing stability to life in New Mexico's villages and small towns. Attempts to have the territory declared a state began as early as 1850, and the idea resurfaced regularly in the following decades, succeeding at last in 1912 despite Eastern concern about the area's poverty and relatively scant natural resosurces—the same conditions that had bothered officials since Oñate's time. Doubts had also been raised by a pronounced cultural diversity, a situation that, ironically, was augmented soon after statehood by the arrival of two distinct new groups of immigrants. Political and

economic refugees, fleeing north by the thousands to excape the uncertainty of life in revolutionary Mexico, formed the larger group; the other consisted of artists, archaeologists, and various other exurbanites, many drawn by the very diversity the good senators had worried about.

Taos and Santa Fe soon achieved a new (and perhaps ambiguous) status as art colonies. Painters, writers, and photographers responded strongly to the Southwest, and the adobe churches, with their striking aesthetic rapport between nature and culture, quickly emerged as a prominent symbol of southwestern traditions. Thousands of images have been based on New Mexico churches since statehood. They might have proved how readily a subject can be reduced to cliché, but the reverse has also happened: the arts have shown how rich in form and association a vernacular architecture can be.

As recognition of the uniqueness and beauty of New Mexico churches widened, so grew the awareness that the churches were more fragile, more vulnerable to neglect than their massive aspects might have suggested. Organized efforts to protect historic buildings and their eroding architectural legacy began as early as 1913 when Dr. Edgar Lee Hewett, director at both the School of American Archaeology and the fledgling Museum of New Mexico, founded a group called the Society for the Preservation of Spanish Antiquities in New Mexico. In 1922, the Committee for the Preservation and Restoration of the New Mexico Missions was formed; its members, including architect John Gaw Meem and writer Mary Austin, took the first decisive steps toward the preservation of historic and architecturally important churches.

The preservation movement's activities had two distinct and equally important effects. In one direction, efforts involved the restorations and protection of historic sites, including the important churches at Acoma, Trampas, Laguna, and the Santuario de Chimayó; in the other, there was a significant revival of mission design elements and use of native materials in new buildings. These efforts helped consolidate the formation of a distinctive regional style, now known rather imprecisely as the Santa Fe style, and encourage its expression in both public and residential architecture.

New Mexico's adobe churches probably reached their greatest geographical and numerical extent in the late 1920s, supported by an agricultural economy in the midst of postwar expansion. Improving yields and markets encouraged small-scale ranchers and farmers to expand their operations (especially plowed

acreage) considerably. At the same time, electricity, mechanization, and road-improvement projects were spreading into far corners of the state. This brief period of relative prosperity brought new churches to small villages and towns, and existing churches were more effectively maintained than in the past.

As always, however, the realities of climate were inescapable. Severe drought across the West combined with the consequences of short-sighted land use to bring on the ravages of the Dust Bowl. The Depression of the 1930s deepened the disaster for New Mexico farmers and ranchers, many only newly brought into the cash economy. Villages were pulled back toward the penury of the past as an overgrazed, overplowed, and overcut landscape seemed to avenge itself.

The combination of drought and economic depression accomplished what drought alone had never quite managed to do, driving people permanently off the land and into towns, cities, and the few agricultural operations with wage-paying jobs. Then, before the Depression had quite ended, World War II called a generation of rural men away to an outside world whose existence most of them had nearly forgotten.

In a very real sense, New Mexicans could not return to the lives they had led before the war. The postwar world was a dramatically different place, with little room left for handmade culture or attempts to farm or ranch a well-sanded, poorly watered landscape. Isolated villages throughout New Mexico almost imperceptibly began to fade away. Their houses, often left furnished at first, ready for a hoped-for return, at last stand empty; slowly overcome by weather and vandalism, they fall into ruin. The churches have tended to resist the decline of their villages longer than the houses around them, standing sentry to abandoned towns long after the last residents have gone.

Historic churches in New Mexico have come to seem as natural, as inevitable to their settings as aspen in mountain meadows or mesquite on the low-lying plains. Yet, like other emblematic elements in the southwestern landscape, their persistence over time is not as certain as it might seem. An era of conservation and preservation has arrived.

This is the ninth year since we started the pilgrimage up the mountain again. It was always a pretty simple thing before. You'd know quite a lot of people gathering at the foot of the mountain, and we just went ahead and walked up.

Then came a time that it seemed like everyone had moved away or had something else they had to do or whatever, but the pilgrimage faded out for a while.

Now that we have it back, it's much bigger than it ever was before. People come from much further away. TV crews show up. Part of the mountain belongs to a corporation, and the pathway crosses the railroad, so we have to have legal releases and insurance and security guards at the tracks. The path, which was always a sort of difficult walk, has been worked on quite a bit so thousands of people can make the walk in a day. Of course, we have an emergency station with medical people and volunteers to patrol the path and so on.

It can seem very strange if you stand among these thousands of people on the day of the walk and think back to what it was. Today people go up with radios and tape players. They run up in jogging shorts. They even manage to get to the top wearing high heels. Every year, the people seem a little less sure of their footing, walking on ground that isn't paved.

And yet, in the most important way, nothing is changed. People have always had their own reasons for coming that are personal, that are different for every one.

Next year will be the tenth anniversary of what you might call the revival of the pilgrimage. I believe there will be ten thousand people. More maybe. If you stay at the bottom, you might not even know it was a pilgrimage. It will be crazy. But for the people who go to the top and stay a while there, it will be the same as in the beginning.

The snow is stopping. If the sky clears off, it's going to be a cold, cold night, maybe around zero. In about 1971, there came a night in January when the temperature went to twenty degrees below zero or worse. Sitting right on top of the wood stoves, practically, people couldn't stay warm. Everyone just stayed in with their families wrapped in coats and blankets and everybody in one room.

Many of the fruit trees were lost that night. Even then, most of the orchards were not used much because it's so easy to get the fruit brought in from out of state. You can't make anything trying to sell the apples when you compete with them. It seems like half the years the frost catches the blossoms in April or May, so you hadn't better count on the trees for anything. The fruit trees are going the way of so many things they had in the past. There was a type of melon with a very thick skin that you could store for months. Also, there were types of corn that were ready to pick faster than what they sell now, that people could use up here where the growing season is short.

Maybe someday if things really get changed around where people need to raise their own food again, we'll see all the crops and orchards back again. I doubt it, though. I think we've seen the last of it, and those few fruit blossoms come out in the spring just to remind us a little of where we came from.

Last week, one of the couples in the village had their fiftieth wedding anniversary. They were both born here and lived their whole lives here, but when it came time to set up the celebration, they rented a hall at the community center down in town, twenty-five miles away. The whole village emptied out. Everybody went. At the time that couple were married, it took two days to get to town. No one would have thought of having a party like that anywhere but here close to home.

That's what it is with the new roads. They're easier, but they change the village and something starts going. Some say tourists and fishermen will start coming up here and maybe the store will reopen. That would be good. But will things ever be what they were before? I doubt it.

That's the road we're on now, and we need to make the best of it. It was a great party, I'll say that. Nobody's forgetting how to celebrate.

I couldn't say just how long the acequia madre has been here. Very few of the oldest houses are still standing, and the church has been changed many times, but the acequia is just about as it always was. It's as much a part of this place as the river and the cottonwoods.

Of course the acequia I remember playing on as a boy was all dirt-sided with old wooden gates. Now most of the acequia is concrete, so less water seeps off into the ground and the ditchbanks don't break through so often. Our headgates are iron and the diversion dam is concrete, so hopefully the floods don't tear things up as bad as they used to. Shovels haven't changed at all, and shovel work doesn't either, but we use machinery when we can.

Things have gotten pretty soft for a mayordomo like me, no? Well, in some ways they are. But no matter how good the ditch is, times always come when there isn't enough water in it—and a dry concrete ditch is no better than a dry dirt one. People start worrying, and calling on the phone, and there's not much you can do. Fortunately, we're upstream where we get the water first, so we're usually alright. A good thing, too—when it gets real dry, worry builds up in the air, just like the dust does.

My family always lived by farming, and my wife's family also; people in the valley used to farm everything you could reach with water. My grandfather once owned most of the fields you can see from here, and when the time came my father and his six brothers and sisters inherited his land.

For many years my brothers used my fields—good land shouldn't lie idle, the land should be used. But I always planned to work that land again myself, and eventually I bought a couple of cows and planted the field to alfalfa. Alfalfa takes a lot of water, and before long I was busy working in the ditch association.

It was a natural thing. The ditch was always my favorite part of my grandfather's land; helping him and my father and uncles with the irrigating never even seemed like work to me. I have known almost everybody in the ditch association for my whole life. But the main thing is that I like life in the valley the way it is, and water is the key to all of it. Quite a few of the fields are only used as pasture now, and some are idle, so the water might seem less important than it once was. But more and more people are coming in here to live—and who can blame them, it's beautiful here—and there isn't enough water for everybody to do everything. Something will have to give.

Farming isn't really the main thing I'm talking about. The land a person owned was important in the past and it's still important, but in New Mexico water and education will make the future, and we have to be sure we've got both those things taken care of.

I'm deep in water politics, but I'd still rather work with the water itself. A day sloshing around in irrigating boots with a

shovel is the most relaxing kind of day I know of. The ditch-cleaning day is often the best, the day in spring that we get everyone out to work together. Well, I can't say everybody; that's the way it used to be. Now people can contribute a few bucks if they'd rather, and we do have expenses, so it's OK. The newer people in the valley often do that. But a large group of us, twenty-five or thirty, start at the headgate and work our way down along the acequia chopping back the shoots of the elms and cottonwoods, clearing weeds and brush, shoveling out the silt and sand piled up since last fall.

It's usually a pretty cold morning. Spring weather, you can't tell just what you'll get, but you have to work hard just to keep warm. By noon it's warmed up and everybody is just a ditch-cleaner, equal, no matter who he is otherwise, and the ditch community is renewed. At the end of the day, if it's not snowing or something, we go down to the old cottonwoods on the riverside and sip a few.

At the end my back says, "So, you are an office worker!" It's true, but I feel like this is my real job. I have been mayordomo of the acequia madre for three years now; I'll do it as long as they want me to. Just come out one fine day in May, see for yourself. Watch the water, and the fish, and the tadpoles pour out onto the fields for awhile, you'll see what it is, it's something real.

People ask where all the old churches are down here in the south, and I can tell you that they're probably all at the bottom of the Gulf of Mexico by now. No matter how big a flood you've seen before, there's a bigger one coming sometime. Our old church had stood on that place at the river bank for almost a hundred years when it came, that great storm.

At first, we tried to use rocks and sandbags, thinking that we might save the camposanto, protect the graves. When the head-stones and crosses started to go, it was terrible. We were afraid of what might become of everything. Before long, though, we saw that the whole camposanto was going to be swept away, and not long after, the flood began to take away the church.

It was really like the end of everything. The fields had all gone, then houses, livestock, everything. The worst came when the water began to take away the bottom of the church. The building shuddered a little, then swayed to one side, and the bell rang. Some of the men started talking about climbing up to save the bell, and others of us had to talk them out of trying it. Soon the water had taken some more of the adobes, and the church leaned over to the other side. The bell rang one more time.

In the end, the church fell into the water all at once and everything was carried off downstream. We rebuilt the church on higher ground, but, you see, the town was gone.

A year without rain. Two years without rain. We've seen it before.

Towns in this low country depend on the creeks, and we do, too, but here we have springs just above the fields, so even if the main part of the creek goes dry, we're still all right. The springs are really what keep us going.

Once in my grandfather's time the springs did go dry and it was a very, very serious thing. No one here could remember anything about the springs ever going dry in all the years since the ancianos first came to this place and were still fighting the Apaches.

Day after day, the men kept going out to those dry fields. There was nothing else really to do but wait.

Well, of course people prayed. My grandmother prayed and promised that if the springs were only to come back, she would make sure that a church would be built here where there had

never been one. It went on for quite some time, and a few of the people left for the season, seeing their crops were certain to fail.

As you see, we are here. The springs did come back. And the church is here, too. My grandmother went out herself to dig the earth for the adobes, and some of the women started to help her. For a long time, it was just the women working while the men went out to try and save the fields and then came back each evening to see what had been done. Finally, the men realized how determined the women were. The church had been promised. It was going up! Then everyone joined into it, and the church was built.

Now the springs are fine, but almost everyone has gone. Yet we keep the church as well as ever. My grandmother's promise must have had a great power. The springs may go, but I think the church will stay.

As you can see here inside the church, we have decided to keep things as they have always been, as we remember them always during our lifetimes, except for a new coat of paint or some new plaster or, of course, new clothes for our santo.

It seems to me that many of the priests in this part of the country are in favor of our way of doing things. We don't see them as often out here as we would like, only once or twice a year, in fact, but there aren't many of us living out here any more as you can see, and it's quite a long drive for the priest coming out over fifty miles on dirt roads to be with us. Though I'll say this, there are always a lot af people here on the day of the fiestas. There are always more people here for the Mass than we have room for inside the church

Last year, we had a large, large gathering, as usual. It was a hot, dry weekend so the roads were especially dusty, but then, on the other hand, the creek had dried up to almost nothing, so people could drive right on down here without getting rides in the back of pickups or walking down.

The procession, where we all escort the saint back into the church, was very nice, and the Mass, too. Then, just at the end of Mass, the priest asked to meet with members of the community for a few words.

Those few words were to say that, in accordance with the

wishes of the church now, barriers between the priest and the parishioners should be removed. What did it mean? He said he wanted us to tear out the altar rail that was older than any of us, that had always been there just as it was.

Well, I can tell you, it created some pretty strong feelings. My neighbor, one of the few people left living down here the year round, started to talk, and he was so upset he couldn't finish what he had to say. He couldn't continue talking! Then the wife of my cousin, a woman whose grandmother helped build the church, stepped in front of the others to say something.

She said, very quiet but stern, "It is a very nice thing that you have come today. It is always a very nice thing to see you on this one day that we see you each year. And it is also very nice to come here to our church, built by our families on lands belonging to them then and to us now, with their own materials, with their own hands, and pray in our church, which is the way they wanted it, with that altar rail as they made it and as it always was. I believe we will all be looking forward when we come next year to seeing you . . . and to seeing this altar rail just as it is. Thank you."

We waited for the priest to say something, but he just shook his head slightly and walked out of the church. We followed. Down the hill, the feast and the music started.

I lived on the West Coast for fifteen years, nine years in L.A., then six in San Francisco, but I always knew I would be coming back. My sister is here, and one of my brothers has moved back, too. My generation of the family spread out all over the country, mostly to Colorado and California, and now we're slowly coming back together.

I was born in the adobe house up there by the road. I thought about moving back into it, but it's not all that big, so I rented it out. Instead, I had some outfit build me this nice frame stucco house. The first week I moved into it, a gust of wind blew the door open and the doorknob went right through the wall! We've given up a lot moving away from the old ways. I should've built another adobe.

I've got my wife and my two sons, both teenagers. A couple of days after we moved in here, I cooked up some fresh eggs that I got from my neighbor for the kids' breakfast. They wouldn't eat them! They said the yolks were too yellow, like there was something wrong with them. They wanted supermarket eggs, with the yolks that were almost white.

I tell you, I got those kids out of the city in the nick of time.

The kids at the middle school decided they wanted to learn more about the history of this area, so the teachers talked it over a while and then put in for a grant to get tape recorders for an oral history project. The grant came through, and soon the kids were going out to talk to people in the valley. They got to choose whoever they wanted to talk to, and they mostly chose the older members of their own families.

One thing that came up was that some kids couldn't talk to their grandparents because some of the older people speak only Spanish or Tewa but most of the kids now speak only English. Parents had to translate across the generations. It was a reminder to me how quiet the traditions can be slipping away and you don't even notice it.

The kids seemed to go out with the idea that the old days were pretty peaceful and easy and now things are messed up somehow. Well, everyone had a fine time talking about the old days, but the more they talked, the less anyone wanted to go back. The kids listened to the viejitos, which isn't the way it always is, and what the viejitos were saying was, there were some hard, hard times.

In Mexico, especially in certain parts of the country, they have saint's days that need celebrating with a fiesta almost every week. That seems like a fine idea to me, but up here we're more into blessings—everything needs to be blessed. We bless babies, houses, cars, pets, you name it.

There's a man here in the village who, when he was younger and cut firewood in the mountains, had his axe blessed each year. Sometimes he would have this done at Christmastime just before he went looking for a Christmas tree in the mountains, sometimes in the spring or some other time of year. I'll tell you this, that was an axe that would sing when he used it.

We always had our fields and water blessed, of course. I remember that some of the priests would stand at one corner of a field and bless the whole thing, but the people liked it to be done another way, especially the cornfields. If the priest walked every row, sprinkling holy water from side to side, he would come back with his cassock dusted with corn pollen, and pollen got spread all over the place. Cornfields blessed that way seemed to do very well.

As you can see, the camposanto, the graveyard here in front of the church, is full. If you look at the dates on the headstones and crosses, you will notice that many of these people died during the influenza that came around World War I, around 1918 I believe. Almost a third of the people at the pueblo died from that sickness.

Today there are a lot of people here that would like to be buried in this churchyard ground when their time comes. The old graves, most of them are so old, I'm sure everything has gone back to the earth. You could bury people here inside these walls again and it wouldn't affect anything. But I guess it won't happen. As you might say, there's no middle ground.

The old churches I knew as a girl had been there so long it seemed that they would always be there. Now so many are abandoned, and some are gone. But my favorite religious place is still there, I'm sure, although I haven't seen it for many years.

Some favorite relatives of my family used to live about thirty miles south of here, down below along the river, and we went often to see them. Every year in May we would go down for the fiestas and the funcion, the celebrations and mass for their town's patron saint. We always left well ahead of time because the shortest way was a steep, rocky road and we liked to be early to help get everything ready. We carried plenty of food and water with us because you never know, and besides extra food would never go to waste on a feast day.

The town had a small church, and also the morada of the penitentes. But the best place was the shrine, where the procession went. The town was by the river, and across the river were high red cliffs, sandstone I suppose. There was a trail to the top of the cliffs, up to the mesa top where the animals grazed; near the top of the trail a narrow path went off to one side along the

cliffs, and this trail led to a place where water seeped out from the rocks into a small amphitheater. That's where the shrine is.

It was such a pretty place, you felt that God must have touched it! A stone wall and juniper branches along the cliffs kept the livestock away, and everything was so green. Spring wildflowers grew there, and thick grass, and it had a grove of small trees so it was sheltered from the wind. The air was sweet and clean, and there were always birds. Among the rocks were votive candles and milagros that the people put, and other things they carried up from below.

You could see out across the valley and far into the distance, over the plowed fields and the fresh green of new leaves on the cottonwood trees along the river. Voices seemed small there, and people were quiet anyway, resting after the climb up. It's hard to remember what the priest said, but it was a place to make you grateful for life.

No one now lives in that town. No one at all. Most of the houses have fallen, or people have taken the stone to build somewhere else. The church is gone too. Several years ago someone came and got the vigas to put in a new roof. But I feel sure the shrine is still there, high on the mesa. Many other things will change, but not a place like that.

The traditional style of building in this area for both houses and the churches was to have a flat roof supported by vigas—beams—that we brought down from the mountains. The favorite wood for the vigas was the pina real, the spruce. It grows tall and straight and even the smaller ones support weight well, which was important because the roofs were a layer of poles across the vigas, then some willows or brush, and then about a foot of dirt put on top. Those roofs were heavy!

Those dirt roofs were the best we could do at the time, but when it was wet they leaked mud and when it was dry they leaked dust. We used a manta, a big piece of muslin, nailed on the ceiling to keep the dust from falling all over everything, and every spring the manta would be taken down and cleaned.

The adobe floors were easier, all you had to do was wet them a little and smooth them out, and there were some things we mixed into the adobe to make the floors last longer.

I believe we had one of the last flat roofs with dirt in this area—this has always been a hard place for farming, and it took us a while to get what we needed for a new tin roof.

When I was a boy, my father was the main one to look after the church. Once when we had been up to southern Colorado to visit part of our family for a couple of weeks, it had been raining here almost every day we were gone, heavy rains. The day after we got back, my father took me with him to go see how things were with the church.

We could see as soon as we walked up to the church how heavy the rains had been. The adobe plaster was washed away here and there, and the winds had blown a cottonwood limb onto the roof. When we went to open the doors, the wood was so swollen by the water that we could barely open them.

When we got them open and saw inside, we just stood there awhile not saying anything. There, growing out of the adobe floor, was a young stand of wheat.

I remember trying to convince my father to leave the wheat alone—it seemed right to me that it should be there—but he just smiled and said, ''Mi hijo, you know we can't worship the wheat.'' In a couple of days, everything was back to the way it was, but I never forgot that day.

The pews we used to have here in the church were all made by hand, and every one was different. We held on to them as long as we possibly could. We never really wanted any others but those. The time came, though, that we couldn't fix them another time. We had to have new ones.

We had a woodworker we knew who lives about fifteen miles from here build us a new set of pews, a complete set. They're really nice, as you can see, but one of the older men in the village came down to look at them and I knew as soon as he came into the church that he was determined to find some reason that the old ones were better.

He looked and looked, and he sat in some of the pews, and you could see he realized that the new ones were very good, that they were probably going to last even longer than the old ones. But as he walked along the aisle one last time, he said, "You know, these new pews are wider than the old ones. It will make it hard." I could see that he was right. The new pews were about six inches wider on both sides of the aisle than before. But so what? He said, "When somebody is carried up this aisle in a coffin, the pallbearers are going to have a hell of a time." It made me a little uneasy to talk about it.

Well, it was true, but he didn't get to see it. As it happened, he was the first person carried through those new benches! That's the way things happen.

San Isidro is our patron saint, the patron saint of farmers. In fact, we have two saints, and they're both San Isidro.

Fifteen or twenty years ago, there was a time of thieves breaking into the churches all over the state and stealing our santos, our carvings and paintings of the saints. I guess they were all being sold to collectors. We started having someone in the village keep San Isidro in their house whenever the church was closed, but there was a problem with that because people would want to go to the church on weekdays, say, and there was no San Isidro. So we got a nice, new, plaster San Isidro, sort of an anglo San Isidro, to stay in the church all the time. Our hand-carved San Isidro just comes out for Mass or a wedding or the feast day.

Now on the feast day, when it comes time for our procession with the santo some people think the old San Isidro should be the true one and others think it's the new one. So now we just have the procession with the two of them.

The rangeland around here gradually got played out. The grass was getting pretty poor already when the Dust Bowl come along, and people started moving away. Some moved to greener pastures, but not many. Most everybody moved into town and took up something different. Still, some stayed.

But out here, things just went from bad to worse. Mesquite's been coming in for quite a while, and it sure looks to do better than beef on this ground. Finally a pretty good flashflood come through and took the houses close to the arroyo, and what was left of the church went down too.

Even after that, though, people would come on back, quite a few at Easter or Memorial Day, to pay their respects at the camposanto, sometimes a bunch on the Fourth of July. Finally some talk got going that we needed a place where people could *get together out here when they came back, so we started col-lecting money, and pretty soon we had concrete picnic tables and trash barrels and soon we'll have a shelter up over some tables so people can get out of the sun or rain if they have to.*

We've had a priest come out to say a mass on the old town's feast day, and now come this next Fourth of July we're going to have the state representative for this area coming out to make a little speech, and I guess he'll talk about the chances of the state helping us take care of this little recreation area we built and maybe adding on to it.

So what do you think of that? There's nobody living out here any more, not a single building with a roof on it. Yet we still have a sort of town here, not a ghost town either. We've still got a community that we belong to.

The house my grandparents built at the foot of Pedernal stood empty for nearly twenty years, and the adobes had started to weather so much that you wouldn't have thought, to look at the outside, that anyone would ever live there again. My parents had moved into Santa Fe, and most of my aunts and uncles had moved away from there too, so nobody needed the old house.

Yet the family never completely abandoned the place. My father kept his grazing permit on the forest lands above there, and he went back whenever he had the chance, always taking us kids with him. Then a few years ago one of my uncles decided to move his family back to that house, so we all went back up there on weekends or summer vacations to help him fix the place up. The inside was still in good shape. There was something important about that house that had never *weathered away, something left from all the years we'd lived there.*

There was an orchard, mainly apple trees, still giving fruit, and with only a little work we got the water running through the ditch again. The house is fine now, and in fact it is that place that feels like the center of the family, not any of the houses in town.

At least once each summer, usually several times, the whole family gathers together up there. I used to spend quite a bit of time there in the summer, but it's very hard to leave it and come back to town, so I don't go as much. When I'm in town, that adobe house and the orchard seem so far away, almost unreal. But then when I'm on the land it's the town that seems even more unreal. This land is magic, though of course being magic it has its demons. But the magic keeps calling me back.

I've got this piece of vega land, field hay, I guess you would call it, that always brings up a good stand of wild grass with a little alfalfa mixed into it. I cut it a couple of times every summer, maybe even three times. Then I use the field as a pasture.

There used to be some grazing permits in my family for the mountain pastures, but the Forest Service has cut back on all the permit numbers over the years. We finally decided it wasn't worth fooling with it. The mountains used to seem like so much land there was enough room for everyone to do what they wanted, but no more. There seems to be a lot of politics mixed up with that permit business, too, and I don't raise cattle as a way of spending time on that kind of thing.

I don't think you can say I'm in the cattle business, as a matter of fact. The way hay prices are these days, I'm sure I could put alfalfa in those fields and just sell it and have nothing to do with the cattle. I'd be able to make a little something on it. I *don't plan on doing that, though. My people, my family, have had cattle now for hundreds of years.*

I raise a few head for the table and my sister gets a couple and there's usually something to trade one for here and there. If I was ever crazy enough to look at what it costs me to raise cows, I might have to switch to bingo or golf for a hobby. We've got rustlers around again these days and punks that'll shoot a cow from the highway just for the hell of it. If you lose one cow that way, you're not in it for the money that year.

The whole thing is really about something else: the feel of a good saddle, the smell of new hay, the sound of water running down a ditch. I'm what they call around here ''mas antes''— somebody who cares about things in the old style. I like trucks and electricity and gas heaters just fine, but I believe you have to spend a certain amount of time tending to your connections with the past or you get lost.

"Dios lo da, Dios la quita"

Throughout much of what was once the Spanish Southwest, stones on the desert and semi-arid lowlands sit motionless in the sun for so long that they darken, as if burned by the ultraviolet light. The landscape in places seems austere even for the stones, yet species adapt and individuals flourish.

Few have done as well as the mesquite, a rugged and tenacious tree the tendrils of whose roots have been found in well corings 750 feet below the surface. Embracing austerity, the mesquite redraws its range year by year, spreading across barren and abused places where few other plants remain.

Contrast and paradox are its element: a subtle honey and bitter smoke come from a plant whose slender leaves are guarded by sharp spines. The mesquite, nearly buried by sand, still puts forth a display of densely-flowered spikes, while below ground its nearly undeterrable taproot drives on toward water. At the surface, deer, coyotes, and mockingbirds shelter in its light shade.

The traces of some other southwestern species lead deep into geological time. On their lifelines the mesquite has only recently arrived. Yet already it looks in some places as if it had always been there and is certain to remain.

W hen the walls of New Mexico's oldest churches were first rising between three and four centuries ago, cartography was still almost an artform—a projection of dreams, legends, and superstitions onto paper.

Chartmakers painted the earliest portraits of the Americas with few facts in hand. Working from sketchy details, their maps were colored by conjecture and intuition, less a documentation of new lands than of widely held hopes and fears of their day. The coasts of their strangely shaped continents were haunted by sea monsters, mines and missions were drawn on the same grand scale as the mountain ranges, and daunting blanks with no features at all stood for vast, unsettling stretches of unexplored country.

Recent maps measure a calculated world in minute increments of precision. Yet certain destinations still seem to call for something from the older approach— some blend of art and objectivity. In isolated corners of the Southwest and along its back roads, the currents of history and a complex interaction of cultures have combined with a diverse landscape to provide an abundant habitat, almost a preserve now, for places that can't be located very well with measurements alone.

The maps that led us to the villages we found best hidden and least known were, in fact, a sort of hybrid. Photocopied sections of fifty- to eighty-year-old county maps, they preserved the tattered and fading features of a vanished state with scarce paved roads, few fences, and an abundance of space left to the imagination. They weren't accurate depictions of the present and had little to offer a traveler in a hurry, yet they weren't really distortions, either; viewed from one perspective, they were like sections of the landscape of history as seen from the air.

Some of these maps led us into narrow valleys, some to sandy barrens dotted with creosote and mesquite, still others onto open plains so vast they could easily hide a church that stood completely alone and in the open. Often, on the other hand, the maps led us to churches that we had breezed by without noticing for years, churches hidden by the deceptive familiarity of their surroundings and the growth of new buildings around them.

The most tantalizing maps usually led to places miles beyond the last crumbling patch of asphalt. Many come to mind, but rather than describe any particular place (since such places insist on a special kind of privacy) I'd prefer to invent one that allows me to recall bits and pieces from those many miles of road. And in homage to the wide-ranging hawks that always watched over us with detached interest, I'll call this town "Gavilan."

The main road toward Gavilan lies along the valleys and low passes of a natural and ancient avenue for travel, traversing the break between high sandstone mesas and a still-higher mountain barrier not traversable by road for many miles. Any attempt to chart its entire history would include the gamepaths and Indian trails, the wagon tracks and railroad grades that have all converged there, as well as the sites of battles, cavalry charges, and mass migrations.

The story has been rich and colorful, but even its most important events made few changes that stand out against the dramatic expanses of the landscape. History has left most of its marks only on the maps. The central concrete fact of travel along the route today is the presence of the route itself—a freeway, stretching visibly ahead for miles, four lanes of fenced pavement that cross the terrain in a sequence of easy, open curves.

Fifteen years ago, the traveler to Gavilan forked off from the main highway into a gathering of well-shaded stone and adobe buildings, the active center of a small hillside community. Close to the village, a few cottonwoods emerged from water hidden in the deep sand of eroded ravines, but piñon and juniper covered most of the ample space of a dry countryside just as they had for centuries. A thin growth of grass and cactus, barely enough to hide a gravelly soil, covered the best of the open ground. On steeper places, even the hardiest grasses and small plants gave way to rocks—and even there, livestock had established well-trod paths, a latticework access to any possible bit of forage.

Fenced pastures and wooden-sided stock pens held a few horses, cattle, sheep, and goats, but there was no farmland in sight. It was ranching country, too hard for any but the most determined of gardeners to plant in. Other than livestock, the only obvious sources of livelihood in the village were a motel and a store, while some faded lettering over the door of an abandoned adobe showed where a third business had been. The freshly painted motel had a couple of patrons parked under its trees, but the store, with a crooked line of pickup trucks and cars outside, was the busiest spot in town. Though small, the store

showed two clear causes for its popularity: there were a couple of multicolored gas pumps out front, as well as the mailbox and flag of a rural post office.

Inside the store, a steady murmur of congenial conversation included a hint or two about the heyday of the town. A trading spot since wagon days, the settlement had taken root at a crossroad where ranchers and villagers from outlying country came to exchange goods and mail. The railroad ran through the center of town, and so did the highway—if it was proper to use the word highway for the meandering track of those times, with hills so steep that early-day car drivers had to gather downhill speed on one to be sure of reaching the top of the next. Poor roads had been one of the trials of life in the area, but they made people grateful to use the closest town for trade and mail, so the town grew. A prominent local figure had headquartered his large ranch here, too, and built a rambling, elaborately furnished hacienda where he once entertained a president. The town had been a busy place for a while. The hacienda was long since gone now, brought down by fire, and sentiment in the store said times like those would not be back. But the tone of those same voices said the town was content to be a quiet place. There were worse fates.

Leaving town, smooth pavement on the side road to Gavilan soon gave way to gravel, then to the ridges and ruts of a straight and narrowing red-clay lane driven through piñon and junipers. The scenery in the rearview mirror disappeared behind a cloud of dense red dust, a fine powder that boiled up from the long straightaway and forced itself into the car to form a thick, tongue-coating red atmosphere. Well-worn shock absorbers and sun-hardened ruts fought for control of the car as a driver searched (again in vain) for the mythical speed that makes a washboard road feel flat. Then suddenly the trees all seemed to stand aside, giving way to an abrupt run of cliffs and an unexpected vista: a thousand feet below lay a small stream, bordered by thin strands of greenery, winding for miles along an open valley floor between sandstone mesas and escarpments.

Old maps showed a string of towns in the country below, tied to each other by that slender thread of water and by the well-beaten road we were on, once an important route to and from the plains beyond. Rock-ridden, edgy, the road pitched down a steep series of grades and switchbacks toward a different sense of place: no longer the high and windblown piñon-juniper grassland that surrounds the mountains, but instead a wide, arid valley floor of red silts and huge sandstone boulders bounded by high walls.

Signs of a settlement, long abandoned, came into view as soon as the road reached level ground. A few courses of stonework nearly hidden by tumbleweed marked one of the first Spanish sites in the valley, built at a narrow, canyon-walled place defensible against Apache and Comanche raiders. The canyon's sheer cliffs had, as hoped, held raiders at bay, but the lingering frost and the cold, damp shadows there were almost as hard on the Spanish farmers and their precarious crops. As soon as raiding stopped, these villagers had moved out to the sunshine of open stretches below. The rough-hewn stones of their abandoned houses were gradually pulled down and used to make corrals, added to rocks once cleared from farmland as fields were given over to pasture. Then the pastures in their turn gave out. A cycle was now completing itself—the stones were moving, almost imperceptibly, back toward their original places on land that was farmland or pasture no more.

The road led past the ruined settlement to the stream, where new and surprisingly large culverts made a ford over its docile flow of clear water. Just below, a stream-built monument of broken concrete, steel, and trees showed why the culverts had to be so big—this trickle had other moods, flash floods charging down out of the mountains every year. Beyond the ford, irrigated fields, mostly planted, set up a brilliant palette in varied tones of green, a vivid contrast to the reds that surrounded them everywhere—in the road, in the sandy soil, and especially along the wet earthen walls that carried the acequia madre's essential, sustaining water.

Nearby stood the first of the valley's still-occupied towns, its pitch-roofed stone houses centered around the traditional plan of a square plaza centered on a church. Yet if this village was, in fact, occupied, it was hard to find evidence at a glance. Even the vacant fields nearby felt more alive. Nothing and no one could be seen to move, in either plaza or houses. The church, unlocked, stood empty except for a few bales of hay stacked near the center of its floor. Pigeons shuffled across the rafters overhead, sometimes beating the air into dust as they flapped out through glassless window frames. As still as it was, though, the town seemed becalmed, not abandoned, a light sleeper whose waking life could only be guessed at.

Even after leaving the town far behind, its air of suspension was only intensified in the valley below, a deep calm unbroken by motion except for the sluggish gait of a slow-moving cow or the distant vigil of ravens and hawks that floated away on warm updrafts. The villages downstream were all deserted. In each, abandoned houses basked in the sun, kept company by their beckoning churches: one whose roof was gone, another with doors and windows nailed shut to defend it against vandals who are the valley's modern raiders. Where the ancient foundations had crumbled, strewn stones were watched over by the weathered crosses and sandstone monuments of *camposantos*.

The road on to Gavilan became rougher by the mile, and active fields were fewer. The stream was weakening. The flow of a southwestern stream is always capricious even in the hands of nature alone. Here there were upstream competitors as well. The water was seldom adequate now to ensure a harvest, and the cycle of farmland to pasture, pasture to weedy barrens had been played out in many places. On a field packed to hard crust by hooves, the brilliant white bones of a horse defeated by winter stood out against red ground. Cottonwood leaves brushed by a light breeze seemed to whisper to preserve the silence, their slight sounds lost in the stillness around them.

Late afternoon brought another ford, with a rocky track beyond that led on to Gavilan. The ford was uncertain; patient, slow-moving water had shaped deep silt into patches of quicksand. Besides, the spell of the valley was strong, insisting on its atmosphere of watchful repose. Why break the silence, the valley seemed to ask, with the sounds of a car mired in shifting mud? Gavilan was used to waiting for its few visitors. It could wait a while longer.

Five years later, the Gavilan drive started with a wider and smoother highway, its new ribbons of blacktop unrolled through a background still beyond the reach of apparent change. New overpasses now occasionally enclosed the view from the road to give drivers a few fast glimpses of landscape framed in nineteenth-century style. Inevitably, the countryside as seen from guard-railed, limited-access roadway seemed a little more remote, a little less real.

The turnoff that led to the Gavilan road had been restructured, and almost hidden, as an inconspicuous option at the nearby freeway exit. Old shade trees over stone buildings looked as stately and sounded as fine as ever with a gentle wind blowing, but their village had been left a little forlorn. Isolated from the curiosity and impulsive stops of passersby, the motel had seen its traffic trickle to nothing. Little noticed and less used by travelers, it had been converted into low-cost apartments. The store still survived, though, with its flag and bright mailbox and array of pickup trucks, apparently unconcerned by the added dents and peeling paint on the veteran gas pumps out front. Crumbling pavement led past town to the dirt road, now a complex of rills and rivulets in slick clay.

The high edge of cliff beyond miles of mud was now the viewpoint into a frost-touched valley. Cottonwoods far below showed autumn color, and a light haze of drifting wood smoke made it possible to pick out the specks that were distant houses. This time, down the road was a steep ramp of rain-loosened stones, probably a good imitation of the wagon track of a century ago where teams and full loads of supplies inched down with the help of taut reins, dubious brakes, and dark imprecations. The prudent driver treated his tires like hooves, feeling out the route a few feet at a time. At last, the car dropped to the level of treetops, then rolled gratefully down the last few yards to the valley floor.

The old ruins and corral, deep in the chill and shadows of the canyon, had conceded a few more stones to the ground nearby. Nature was reasserting itself quietly there, and the pace of change was almost imperceptible. The ford below was another matter: some recent flood had tossed aside its concrete and culverts, leaving behind a treacherous chaos of boulders, mud banks, and murky waterholes. A high-wheeled wagon and a surefooted team are probably better than a car for a place like that, and it brought to mind the sight of Navajos working their way up Canyon de Chelly behind horses. But there was no wagon to be had, just muddy tracks that led in and out of a dubious crossing. The fording point was a series of sandstone ledges hidden underwater. The exhaust pipes and muffler erupted in clouds of steam, tires spun, the car frame twisted and groaned, but the car sputtered out onto the far bank and drove on.

Fallow fields just below the ford outnumbered the green now. Idle plots of tall, yellowing grasses framed the trim acres between them, where the year's last cutting of hay stood stacked in bales. The fields waited for the oncoming season of rest, but the village close by, so inert before, was awake. Chickens stalked seeds in the old plaza, goats and horses gazed indifferently at the passing car, and dogs rushed off porch stoops to sound an alarm as we drove slowly into their territory.

The church was completely transformed. It carried a new coat of plaster, its foundations had been reinforced with concrete and refaced with stone, and the windows were all reglazed. Its doors, freshly painted, were closed and locked to protect the space inside. Knocking at houses where stone chimneys showed smoke, we soon found the *mayordomo*, the person responsible for looking after the church. We stood talking on a porch decked with harnesses, traps, axes, and a basket of loose tractor parts. After a few minutes of cautious conversation, the church doors were unlocked and we stood in the nave that had been strewn with straw five years before.

For the *mayordomo*, the lives of the church and village shared something important with the life of an individual—"The first hundred years are the hardest." He mentioned Indian raids, drought, and mountain lions. Massive church beams had been cut in the mountains more than thirty miles away and dragged down into the valley behind teams of horses to be part of a structure built strong enough to withstand armed attack. The church had seemed huge

and mysterious to him as a boy, and its mysteries had been part of everyday life. His mother had insisted that the family go pray early each day "before God gets too busy." He described the tolls once collected from steady wagon traffic on the valley road and the busy lives and work of members of his family—trapper, postmaster, farmer, nun. Life in the valley had always been far from amenities and close to the force of the elements, but it had been a life among large families, many friends, and much sharing.

Newer times had brought new trials. Above all, there was the growing, thirsty city upriver that captured so much of the normal flow of the stream and replaced it with effluent from a water treatment plant. Villages below it had been drying up, one by one, slowly drained not only of water but of population. Decades ago, the people started going in and out of the valley as migrant farm workers. Now they left to find permanent jobs and livable wages. Many went, like the water, to the city nearby; others were dispersed all across the country, but a few returned.

Yet the village and the church had not been forgotten, even by a generation scattered from Seattle to Miami. The day came when the aged church, no longer used, had to be either renovated or pulled down, if only to protect the safety of children playing around it. The few remaining villagers debated, and the word went out to friends and relatives that support was needed. The decision made to restore the church was not easy, and neither was the work: old adobe exposed to rain and snow weathers quickly, while walls that will last are slow to rise. Contributions of supplies, money, and labor soon got rebuilding under way, and it was done *mas antes*—done with care, in the old ways that restored the spirit of the church as well as its structure.

Standing outside again as the church was locked, we asked about the road through to Gavilan. Rough now, he said, since so few people lived down that way that the county crews rarely touched it. A large ranch had to be crossed on the way, and it had posted stern warning signs that suggested the road was private, a response to cattle rustled or shot. "You will bump into some old acquaintances of mine down there—big rocks," he said, "but if you want to go badly enough, you can get there."

An hour and several good scrapes later, we stood at the second ford ready to cross when an old pickup came into view, slowed down at the sight of us, then lurched slowly in our direction. It wasn't long before the truck pulled up behind us at the ford and the driver climbed out, his door swinging open with the dusty grinding noise common to all veteran desert hinges. The driver looked like he had been in the Southwest at least as long as the truck, and he had boots, gloves, and hat to match. It turned out he had been born about fifty yards from where we stood, in an adobe house that was little more now than a high mound of earth with some splintered timbers poking out of it. He was down from the city on this day to look after a few cows and "just spend a couple of hours with the old place." What about Gavilan? "It's empty now, way back past locked gates. If you want to go there, you'll have to talk to someone from that family, and the closest of them lives above in the city now." We wrote down a name or two, shook hands with the cowboy, and backed away from the ford. We left with those names in our pocket that might lead, next time, to Gavilan.

That next time was to be another five years later, a trip made over the objections of a restless, blustering spring. Driving again past fading roadside towns, we now passed by the Gavilan turnoff as well. Seen from the highway, the village at the junction looked nearly deserted: the store and its post office had been closed, while no more than three or four of the nearby houses, either under the trees or out on the hillsides, appeared to be occupied.

We followed the highway through the mountain's sprawling foothills this time, to the city beyond. We had arranged to meet the *mayordomo* of Gavilan's church and follow him out to the town that had proven so elusive. The *mayordomo* was a direct but soft-spoken man with a face deeply lined by years of sun and wind. He and his wife invited us into a long L-shaped adobe with a full-length *portal* supported on carved and painted beams. Each room of the house had a door onto the *portal*, and doors and windows alike were trimmed with the traditional, protective blue of the cloak of the Virgin of Guadalupe. Inside, wide interior window ledges were filled with flowering geraniums, the rich orange of their petals in perfect concert with the color of sunlit adobe. Family portraits in wooden frames and images of saints shared the ledges, walls, and the lace-covered tops of tables and cabinets.

Invited into the kitchen for coffee, we sat near two cook stoves placed side by side. One was a modern gas range, but the other, at least fifty years old, was fueled by wood. Because the morning's spring air still had an edge, coffee was simmering over the woodstove's radiant fire of juniper and pine. A calendar near the coffeepot showed bemused whiteface beef chewing on the greenery of some pastoral paradise, which led to talk of the cattle business. Beef prices were falling, our hosts remarked with a quiet irony, but spring rains were not—it was beginning to look like business as usual again this year.

Outside, the winds of March were rising. We reluctantly left the house and its beguiling warmth behind and were soon following the *mayordomo*'s pickup down an unfamiliar road toward Gavilan. The road crossed miles of rolling, open land bordered by barbed wire fences and telephone lines. Behind us, fast-moving patterns of storm light and shadow fortified the haughty grandeur of the mountains. Ahead, power poles and windmills were the loftiest features of the terrain, towering over land trimmed close to the ground by cattle and wind. Hawks perched on the poles ignored us as we drove by, intent on their hunting in the tall, ungrazed grasses of the roadside.

We quickly covered the paved stages of this new approach, since its roads (and most roads east of here for a thousand miles) were laid out in the relentless straight lines and right angles that spread so readily over flat land. But these neat lines led again to abrupt cliffs and an immense vista. The pitch forward into the valley was relatively gentle, easier than the steep series of crumbling switchbacks we had confronted five years earlier, but it was still a descent of nearly a thousand feet, a downglide that ended with a touch of the surprise that is part of a light-aircraft landing.

The grade had dropped into a wider, more open part of the valley than before, and the road below was better. The pickup sped easily ahead over ground as familiar to our guides as their own driveway in town. We soon reached a ford— the same one that had kept us away from Gavilan twice before, a place with a certain familiarity for us now, too.

The pickup had crossed and was almost out of view, so we waded in after it. Under ominous black silt there was a hidden footing of stone, and after dropping briefly into just a hole or two for drama, the ford was behind us. The road on was as rough and rock-strewn as it looked from across the river, but it wasn't far to the gate we had heard about, already unlocked and open. Today's journey would reach Gavilan!

The road climbed away from the valley floor in an intricate pattern of curves, evading the grasping fingers of an arroyo that reached toward it on the right. Nearby to the left, sets of washed-out ruts and parallel gullies showed where earlier generations had made their way to Gavilan in wagons and trucks. Now the road rose gradually into a low pass in the piñon-covered sandstone ridge ahead. It skirted one last hillside curve, and we were there.

We first saw Gavilan almost as the old maps did, in a view from the ridge above that emphasized how small a place it was, how secluded by the expanses of rugged, beautiful terrain around it. A painterly array of red hills formed the immediate background, hills bounded in turn by towering mesas whose remote crown of ponderosa pines seemed tiny from below. A steep-walled red arroyo carved its way out of the mesas' cliffs and down through the town in the same series of sinuous arcs shown on the map. There was, however, one striking difference between the map's view and ours: the town was now deserted, and at least half of the buildings once shown there were gone.

Gavilan had obviously been a cow town, surrounded as it was by old corrals and stock pens and showing no trace of fields or acequias. The arroyo nearby was deep, but it was one of those sometimes-dry, sometimes-flooded channels so common in the Southwest, usually wet enough to water livestock, but no source of the long-lasting, steady flow needed for irrigated farming. The houses on its banks were built close together, not for defense, as in other valley towns (Gavilan was established after Indian raids had ceased), but because their hand-dug wells held them close to reachable water.

Water had written much of the history of Gavilan, but not all. Once-open low-lying country had gradually been fenced in, increasing the pressure on sparse rangelands, while wind and water erosion steadily undercut the ability of heavily grazed land to recover. Finally, changes in the cattle market and competition from better-suited land brought the story of Gavilan as a community to a close. Its natural beauty and tranquility still remained, however, surrounding the one building in town left substantially intact by time—the church.

The *mayordomo* walked up to meet us at the churchyard gate. He held a coil of rusty barbed wire and a fencing tool in one gloved hand, unhooking the gate from its wire loop with the other and pushing it open. A narrow flagstone pathway, nearly hidden by tall, wild grasses that brushed at our knees, led to the doors of a church whose trim exterior gave little hint of the building's age. The doors recently had been repainted, their brilliant white dramatically set off by large, black cast hinges and a brass padlock.

The doors opened on an interior that, regardless of the actual age of the church, was *mas antes*—an expression of conservative spirit centering on a preservation of tradition and style. As our eyes adjusted to the low light, telling details emerged: the *santos*, pews, and altar railings, all handmade; a woodstove, polished and gleaming as if it had been made yesterday, but dating, in fact, to the turn of the century; light fixtures, both overhead and mounted on the walls, that were ornate oil lamps sheltered by a building still untouched by electricity; and spruce vigas that still bore the marks of axes and adzes.

Yet these elements, as attractive as they were, nonetheless played a subordinate part. They were grace notes that had harmonized with place and use to create a more pervasive feeling, and it was the concert of them all—the religious dedication of the architecture, the surrounding terrain, and a history with myriad levels—that made this feeling distinctive and remarkable.

We stayed quite a while, walking slowly through the church as the *mayordomo* pointed out the favorite details. For him, most of the church's furniture and fixtures evoked thoughts of the individuals and families that had contributed them. His own family had done a great deal for this church, and his knowledge of the building was so thorough, expressed with such ease, that in telling its story he might well have been describing the personalities in a gallery of family portraits.

At one point we stopped in front of a tall, mullioned, double-hung window; its wooden frames, so far from modern styles, appeared to be as old as the church. As we looked through one toward the mesas in the distance, we realized that each of its many panes was different; some were recent, a few may have been original, the rest dated from the many years in between. Ripples, creases, and colors altered the appearance of the landscape outside. Taken together they formed a mosaic more intricate, yet more expansive, than the view through any one pane.

Bob finally set up a tripod, fixed his camera in place, and resumed once more a process whose aimed-for result would resemble one of the views through those panes: part of a mosaic of something that a single view couldn't comprehend.

Some time later we locked the doors behind us, walking on to the venerable length of juniper that served as a gatepost. Worn to a smooth, comfortable surface by the many hands that had rested on it over the years, its warmth now seemed to invite us back just as plainly as had the *mayordomo* and his wife.

On the way back to the city we realized that the red-clay road had become familiar, sympathetic, part of the experience we had sought. Gavilan had become part of our personal histories, of the landscape we thought of as home.

NOTES ON PLATES

PAGE 1. *Church and Graveyard, Mimbres Valley, 1976.*

The graveyard is highlighted in the foreground by its thick cover of grasses. Well fenced, the cemetery is the only ungrazed land in this view and now provides an inadvertent range sample. The bleached bones of a dead cow lie on the ground just outside the fence.

The storm clouds here are approaching Cook's Peak, a landmark for stagecoach drivers and other travelers on the Butterfield Trail.

PAGE 2. *Abandoned Church, near Black Mesa, 1987.*

PAGE 3. *Church and Meadows, Los Ojos, 1987.*

PAGE 4. *Church and Camposanto, San Rafael, 1986.*

PAGE 5. *Oratorio, Las Palomas Creek, 1986.*

This private chapel is on the nearly abandoned townsite of San Miguel.

Las Palomas is Spanish for "the doves," which in this landscape would refer to the mourning doves whose soft call, though melancholy, is a cheering sound in the desert as an indication of nearby surface water.

PAGE 6. *Church Bell, Lower Anton Chico, 1986.*

The Pecos River Valley, near Anton Chico, was first settled by the Spanish in the 1820s. In 1841, during their ill-fated attempt to capture New Mexico, a column of Texans marched by this particular place.

PAGE 10. *Hand-carved Door, San José de la Laguna, 1975.*

Historians believe that members of several Rio Grande pueblos fled the Spanish reconquest of New Mexico in 1696 by retreating to the Pueblo of Acoma. These refugees moved again in 1697, accompanied by some of the Acomas themselves, to found the pueblo of Laguna. They chose a site on hills that overlooked a large, long-established beaver pond, or "laguna," located on the Rio San José.

Construction of this church, built of abundant nearby stone rather than of adobe, was begun in 1706 or 1707.

PAGE 12. *Feast Day at Laguna, 1988.*

San José is carried at the head of a procession through the pueblo.

PAGE 16. *Shrine in Candlelight, San Lorenzo, 1986.*

PAGE 18. *Morada, Overlooking the Rio Chama, 1987.*

This building represents two parallel revivals. One is the resurgence of the Penitente Brotherhood, which as recently as a decade ago seemed destined to disappear; the other is a strong renewal of interest and pride in traditional New Mexican architecture and its techniques.

PAGE 23. *Los Hueros, at the Foot of Le Febres Mesa, 1986.*

French placenames such as "Le Febres" are fairly common east of the Sangre de Cristos, many a legacy of the French trappers and traders who roamed the area in the early 1800s. *Los Hueros* means "the fair ones," or "the blondes."

PAGE 27. *The Mission of Quarai, 1990.*

The great mission of *La Purisima Concepción de Cuarac*, known more recently as Quarai, was built to serve a population of some five hundred Tiwa-speaking Pueblo people. Archaeologists believe the site was first occupied between A.D. 1300 and 1350 and was probably involved in a salt trade centered at nearby saline lakes.

In the late 1660s, residents of the pueblo planned a joint rising with Apaches to drive the Spanish out, but this effort was discovered and its leaders were executed. Not long after, Apache attacks combined with drought and disease to weaken Quarai and its neighboring pueblos beyond the point of viability. By the end of the 1670s these pueblos were abandoned. The Spanish made attempts to reoccupy the area as early as the 1750s; Quarai was resettled in or about the year 1800.

The impressive ruins at Quarai, as well as those of Abó and Gran Quivira, are now part of Salinas National Monument.

PAGE 28. *Shrine of the Hermit, 1975.*

Hidden from view near this cross is the cave of the hermit Juan María Agostini, described by local legend as an Italian aristocrat who became disillusioned with worldly life and sought to live out his days in seclusion.

His solitude and his care for the poor and sick soon gained him a reputation as a holy man, as well as the attention he had sought to avoid. He soon moved from a cave near Romeroville to this place, high on the sheer granite cliffs of the *Cerro del Tecolote*— Owl Peak. Still his reputation brought followers and curiosity seekers.

In about 1868 he left this cave and started south, probably toward Las Cruces, but before he reached his destination he met a violent death under circumstances that are still argued about. The mountain he had lived on came to be called *Monte Solitario*, in his memory. Today it is known as Hermit's Peak, and his cave is still sought out by pilgrims.

PAGE 31. *Storm at San Pedro Church, Chamita, 1987.*

Chamita, located between the Rio Grande and the Rio Chama and almost within sight of Oñate's 1598 settlement, may have been occupied by Spanish colonists nearly that early. A formal grant was conferred on settlers at Chamita in 1724.

PAGE 34. *San Lorenzo de Picurís Mission, 1987.*

Picurís Pueblo is believed to have been the largest of the northern pueblos in 1680, with a population of nearly three thousand. After Pueblo resistance to the Spanish collapsed in 1696, the people of Picurís fled to the plains to live among the Apaches. When they returned to their ancestral lands in 1706, after sixteen years of struggle with the Spanish and ten years on the plains, there were fewer than three hundred left. For the last century the population at Picurís has averaged scarcely a hundred persons.

In 1769 Comanches destroyed the predecessor of the mission pictured here, which may be the fifth built at the pueblo. Efforts to preserve this longest-lasting of Picurís missions came dramatically to an end in March of 1988, when its structurally weakened walls were pushed over. Soon after the site was cleared, the people of Picurís started work on yet another adobe church.

PAGE 35. *Capilla de San Miguel at El Valle, c. 1976.*

Amid heated controversy, this church, weakened by moisture behind its stucco plaster and by other structural problems of long standing, was torn down in 1985. The buttresses in this view, quite large in proportion to the building, are symbolic of the long struggle to preserve the building. Construction of a new church was completed in 1987.

PAGE 36. *Abandoned Church, Lower Rio Gallinas, 1975.*

PAGE 37. *Collapsed Morada, along the Rio Puerco, c. 1976.*

Visible between the fallen *vigas*, or ceiling beams, are the traditional split-cedar *latillas* that were used in New Mexican architecture from at least Oñate's time until well into the twentieth century, and whose use is now being revived as an element of adobe construction. The *vigas* and *latillas* here once supported a flat roof covered with as much as a foot of dirt.

PAGE 38. *Stone-cut Shrine, Pajarito Plateau, 1989.*

Ancestors of Pueblo people who now live along the Rio Grande occupied the Pajarito Plateau for roughly three centuries, from about A.D. 1250. After the Spanish were driven out of New Mexico in 1680, some Pueblos returned to the Plateau to build villages they could defend if and when the Spanish came back. This shrine was carved into the rock near one such refugee pueblo.

PAGE 39. *Chancel Ceiling, Laguna, 1986.*

The sanctuary of San José de Laguna, unlike most of its counterparts among Pueblo missions, is so ornately painted that the structure and materials of its walls are nearly hidden. Members of the pueblo have, from time to time, retouched the painting with colors ground from native materials.

PAGE 43. *Private Chapel, Cieneguilla, c. 1976.*

This chapel stands on the ruins of a major pueblo, also known as Cieneguilla, that was abandoned around 1680. It was built as a morada, then later became a family chapel. For many years Spanish settlers who lived below La Bajada Hill came to this place as pilgrims on Good Friday.

PAGE 46. *Church, Moquino, 1975.*

Moquino is a small community located in isolated, roughlooking country distinguished by the eroded necks of extinct volcanoes. The area has changed so little that, except for the pristine white propane tank beside the church, this view might be mistaken for one made by A.C. Vroman in the mid-nineteenth century.

PAGE 48. *Camposanto, Galisteo, 1974.*

Galisteo was probably first seen by Spaniards in 1581 as the center of a large population of Tano-speaking Pueblo people. A Franciscan mission was established there sometime before 1629.

Galisteo Basin warriors were prominent during the warfare of 1680, and the Spanish refused to let them reoccupy this area after the reconquest. Comanche raids soon changed the official outlook, however: the Tanos were ordered back to the basin to take the brunt of attacks. This repatriation soon failed: Comanches, smallpox, and the poor harvests of a Tano generation untrained in farming in the old ways drove the Pueblos out of the Galisteo Basin for good.

Spanish settlers later brought cattle to the basin, and a small trading center slowly emerged beside Galisteo Creek. The cities of the Pueblo warriors slowly disappeared under grass and hoofprints.

PAGE 51. *Snowstorm, Bernal, 1987.*

This church is on the Santa Fe Trail, and its village of Bernal was once a stagecoach stop. The peak in the background to the left of the church (usually surmounted by a cross) is Starvation Peak, which local legend says was named after an incident in which 120 Spanish colonists were trapped there by Indians and gradually starved.

PAGE 53. *San Miguel, 1989.*

This *santo de bulto* of San Miguel (Saint Michael) was probably made in about 1850, the work of the mid-nineteenth-century *santero* Rafael Aragon.

PAGE 54. *Crosses, Tomé Hill, 1975.*

Tomé Hill probably has been the site of religious objects and activities for many centuries. A dark, rugged outcrop of volcanic rock, it lies in country along the Rio Grande that was occupied before the Spanish *entrada* by pueblos of the Southern Tiwa. These pueblos would almost certainly have involved Tomé Hill in their religious activities, probably regarding it as sacred and referring to it in Pueblo legends.

At the time of the Pueblo Revolt the pueblos in the vicinity were abandoned, never to be reoccupied by the Tiwa. In 1739 the land below Tomé Hill was granted to *genizaro* and Spanish

settlers whose descendants still form part of the annual Good Friday procession to the hilltop.

PAGE 57. *Easter Pilgrims near Chimayó, 1988.*

The valley of the Santa Cruz River at Chimayó once contained so many private shrines and chapels that it was known as *El Valle de las Capillas*—the Valley of the Chapels. Chimayó in its early days was on the eastern frontier of Spanish New Mexico, frequently attacked by Comanches and others, and the village developed as a collection of defensible, semi-enclosed plazas, many with chapels incorporated or close by.

An annual Easter pilgrimage to one of the Chimayó chapels, the *Santuario*, has been taking place for over a hundred years. Today, Easter pilgrims are drawn to the *Santuario* from places far beyond New Mexico, traditionally crossing as many of the last miles as possible on foot.

PAGE 58. *Cristo Rey Procession, 1987.*

Monte Cristo Rey is the highest of the rugged hills where New Mexico, Texas, and Mexico meet—a dramatic vista-point over the Rio Grande and to distant desert ranges on both sides of the international boundary.

For the last fifty years there has been a procession to the mountaintop on the last Sunday in October, culminating in an afternoon ceremony at the foot of the massive cross on the mountaintop.

PAGE 60. *Santuario de Chimayó, Good Friday, 1988.*

In Tewa tradition the site of the *Santuario* has always been a source of strong healing forces and the destination of important religious journeys; early Spanish settlers continued the ancient custom of traveling to the place.

The chapel built over the Tewa shrine in 1816 was dedicated to Our Lord of Esquipulas, patron saint of another famous and ancient healing place in Guatemala. At that distant site, whose springs and earth are held sacred by the Maya, a bishop cured during a major epidemic in 1737 erected one of the largest cathedrals in Central America. The widely known Guatemalan image of *Nuestro Señor de Esquipulas* appears to have been the model for the one still in place at Chimayó.

The origins of the name "Esquipulas" have been hidden by

time. Some say the word derives from the Mayan, possibly from a term meaning "place of the rising waters." Others have said that Esquipulas was an Indian leader who surrendered peacefully to the arriving Spaniards.

The Greek and Roman god of healing was known as Aesculapius. His temples were in sacred groves, near medicinal springs, and on mountain crests. Sites dedicated to him were places of cure, and pilgrims left offerings of thanks and votive tablets at those shrines.

PAGE 61. *Pilgrims Arriving at Chimayó, 1987.*

Pilgrims who successfully complete their intended journey to the *Santuario* on Good Friday often leave behind their walking sticks and staffs, or some other token of the event, in or near the chapel.

PAGE 63. *Cordova during Las Posadas, 1987.*

Las Posadas, celebrated in the nights before Christmas, is a reenactment of Mary and Joseph's search for lodging among the inns — *las posadas* — of Jerusalem. The drama derives from the days of the *autos sacramentales*, religious plays arranged by Franciscan missionaries to portray events from the Bible for non-readers.

Lit outside by the *luminarias* and *farolitos* so familiar in New Mexico's Christmas, and often inside by candlelight, a church at *Las Posadas* has an atmosphere that is uniquely its own.

PAGE 65. *Capilla de Dolores, Cuarteles, 1987.*

The holiday lights and newly trimmed tree seen here combine with a traditional blue-painted ceiling vault to make the *Capilla de Dolores* look especially festive, fully decked out for Christmas.

PAGE 66. *A Mayordomo at the Door of His Church, Ojitos Frios, 1986.*

PAGE 69. *Upper San Isidro, 1986.*

This aerial view of Upper San Isidro shows many elements characteristic of villages throughout New Mexico. The village stands near reliable water (in this case the Pecos River); its houses are close to the farmable land, and also close enough to the water level of the valley floor to make hand-dug wells feasible — yet no houses have been built on cropland. Fields are more-or-less perpendicular to the stream, giving each access to the ditch on its high end and to the river below; most tracts have been reduced to narrow strips by land-splitting for inheritance.

A steeple below and left of center marks the church, which stands at the center of what remains of a plaza. Downriver (closer to the viewer), a *morada* stands isolated for privacy, with its own *camposanto* beside it.

The village is close to the mountains, so its houses need pitched roofs; yet the climate is still mild enough that shallow pitches will serve. Beyond the village a road leads toward the mountains, though visibly trailing off. Firewood would always have been relatively close by here, and snow pushes cows down out of high summer pastures of their own accord.

Beyond lie mountain pastures, game, and fish.

PAGE 71. *Acequia and Church, Puerto de Luna, 1989.*

PAGE 73. *Oratorio, Casa Salazar, 1989.*

Wagon wheels in the foreground are a reminder of how recently buckboards were still in use in New Mexico, especially on and near the Navajo Reservation.

PAGE 74. *Interior, Las Trampas, 1975.*

This mission at Las Trampas, completed before 1776, is one of the finest surviving examples of Spanish Colonial architecture in the Southwest.

The church is known more completely as *San José de Gracia del Rio de Las Trampas*. "Del Rio de Las Trampas" translates roughly as "on the trapstream," a reference to the site of its settlement on a once beaver-laden watershed. Structurally threatened as recently as 1986, the church is now included in a number of comprehensive preservation plans.

PAGE 75. *Side Altar of Santo Niño Chapel, Chimayó, 1974.*

PAGE 76. *Interior at Cuchillo, 1986.*

The small community of Cuchillo sits on Cuchillo Negro Creek, an often-dry tributary of the Rio Grande near Truth or Consequences that was once a favorite haunt of Apache bands.

This church was built to replace a larger one destroyed by a flashflood more sudden and violent than any the town's residents could remember. The flood stripped away much of the farmable land at Cuchillo and replaced it with sand, and homes were lost as well. Many residents moved away, but the town refused to die and the church was soon rebuilt.

PAGE 77. *Abandoned Church, Restored to Use as a Shrine, 1989.*

PAGE 79. *A pilgrim on the Mountains, 1987.*

PAGE 81. *Procession at Cieneguilla, 1976.*

The feast day at most New Mexico churches is marked by a procession such as the one shown here. A community of friends and neighbors with ties to Cieneguilla reunites each year to celebrate the feast of San Antonio with the traditional guitars, bonfires, and shotguns fired into the air.

PAGES 82, 83. *Procession, Tortugas, 1987.*

The residents of Tortugas are descendants of Pueblo villagers who retreated from New Mexico with the Spanish during the rising of 1680. Those ancestors settled Ysleta del Sur near El Paso in about 1850. For reasons that are no longer known, a smaller group left Ysleta del Sur and, setting something of a precedent for a Pueblo group by moving towards the north, settled Tortugas village near Las Cruces.

This procession starts at dawn at the end of an all-night vigil. Its pathway was once through sandy arroyos, across open desert of creosote bush and mesquite, and up a rugged unmarked mountainside; today's pilgrims cross under an Interstate Highway, walk along a flood diversion channel, and climb a mountain whose access road leads to microwave and television transmission towers. Yet these transformations seem to have little effect on the pilgrims, some of whom have been making this journey annually for nearly fifty years.

As the pilgrims walk, many gather yucca wands to form tall, often ornate blazons, called *quirogas*, to carry with them up the mountain. The procession spreads out as people make their way to the mountaintop throughout the day, and in the afternoon a Mass is said.

By dusk, the pilgrims have all descended the mountain. Just after nightfall the procession returns to Tortugas village, the pilgrims emerging from the foothills in an almost silent column on a path lit by bonfires. They arrive at one last, great bonfire in front of the church, where they place their shining yucca lances.

PAGE 89. *Blessing of the Waters, Valdez, 1987.*

Fields in a drought-haunted landscape are constantly at risk, and farmers in New Mexico villages and pueblos have always made every possible effort to ensure the flow of water. Antecedents of this ceremony certainly reach back thousands of years in the Southwest, further in other parts of the world. Blessings and other rites in New Mexico have centered not only on rivers and wells, but on the ditches and fields as well.

PAGE 91. *Camposanto, amidst Ruins of San Geronimo de Taos, 1975.*

Several attempts to establish a mission at Taos Pueblo during the seventeenth century ended with either buildings or foundations in ruins. The walls seen here were probably erected in 1706 after the previous church was destroyed in the era of Pueblo-Spanish warfare and the Spanish reconquest.

In 1847, during a rebellion against American officials who just recently had taken control of New Mexico, a number of insurgents realized they had failed and took refuge in the church. When they refused to surrender to a detachment of American troops under Col. Sterling Price, he brought forward artillery and reduced the church to ruins once more.

Construction of yet another church, which is currently in use, was started in 1847 or 1848.

PAGE 93. *Prayer on a Feast Day, 1987.*

PAGE 95. *Shrine to the Virgin of Guadalupe, Monte Cristo Rey, 1986.*

PAGE 97. *Restored Church, Lower Rio Gallinas, 1986.*

This is the same church pictured on page 36, just over ten years later. In the worst cases, an adobe church can fall utterly to ruin within ten years of abandonment; here the reverse has happened. This church, restored largely through the efforts of a single extended family, is an outstanding example of traditional New Mexican church architecture.

PAGE 99. *Restoration, Ranchos de Taos, 1987.*

The Mission of San Francisco de Assisi south of Taos, certainly the most painted and most photographed piece of architecture in New Mexico, has become something of a cultural icon—known well beyond the borders of New Mexico as a symbol of the Spanish Southwest. This is due in part to famous images, including those of Paul Strand and Georgia O'Keeffe, but even more to the people of Ranchos whose determination to maintain the original design of the church is the source of its strength as a symbol.

The parishioners at Ranchos have been extremely reluctant to modify the building in any way. The most obvious changes at the church have been additions to the buttresses, enlarged gradually over more than two hundred years.

The last major modernization at the mission was an application of concrete plaster, intended to save the trouble of recoating the exterior with adobe every year; the result was that moisture from leaks was trapped under the plaster shell, and the walls' ancient adobes began to revert to the pile of earth they came from. In time it was obvious that the "improvement" threatened the structure.

Today the concrete plaster is gone, replaced with the adobe that served so well for generations. The surface of the mission is once again changing continuously, while the spirit of the place scarcely changes at all.

PAGE 101. *View toward the Altar, Cañoncito, 1985.*

The tin ceiling here is a striking example of the integration of modern materials with older, more traditional elements.

PAGE 103. *Santos on a Side Altar, 1974.*

PAGE 106. *Danzantes Forming, Bernalillo, 1987.*

The precise origins of the Matachines dance have been lost, probably hidden among the histories of the Moors in Spain and the Spanish in Mexico. Whatever its roots may be, every group that performs this dance imparts a distinct and individual character to it. Initially (perhaps) a Spanish ceremony, the Matachines ceremony in New Mexico has also been adapted by the Pueblos and imbued with additional symbolic colorations.

Complex and ambiguous, the meaning of the dance today lies in the eyes of the beholder. A whip-wielding bull, innocence incarnate in a white lace dress, and a decrepit old man fiddling strident notes combine with ranks of masked dancers to evoke moods of devotion, violence, mystery, and exaltation.

PAGE 107. *Fiesta Princesses, 1987.*

PAGE 110. *Capilla de San Miguel, La Puente, 1987.*

La Puente was named for an old bridge, no longer standing, over the Rio Chama.

PAGE 111. *Church and Abandoned Schoolhouse, Trujillo, 1986.*

Trujillo, founded about 1836, sits at the edge of the Canadian Escarpment whose sandstone cliffs and bluffs form part of the western rim of the Great Plains. Once an area of extensive farming and ranching, the meadows and low ridges above the escarpment have gradually fallen idle. Today the landscape is scattered with sandstone ruins that look almost like natural formations. The schoolhouse and homes that formed the old plaza at Trujillo are all abandoned, but the stone church, faithfully maintained, is still in regular use.

PAGE 114. *Camposanto, near the Punta de la Mesa de San José, c. 1976.*

PAGE 115. *Descanso, 1990.*

Descansos, memorials placed by relatives or friends at the site of a death, have been a common sight along New Mexico roadways for many years. A little over a decade ago, however, they started to become scarce—partly because the more ornate ones had begun to be collected as a folk-art form. Today they are once again frequently seen, distinctive *momentos mori*.

PAGE 116. *Pilgrims among the Mesquite, Monte Cristo Rey, 1987.*

PAGE 119. *Church, Salitral, 1990.*

PAGE 121. *Cubera, 1975.*

PAGE 122. *Road from the Old Ford, San Augustin, 1975.*

The road through this place, difficult to build and maintain partly because of the steep sandstone cliffs of the Canadian Escarpment nearby, was operated as a toll road for many years.

PAGE 127. *Abandoned Chapel, Rinconada, c. 1976.*

The light-diffusing fabric seen hanging from the ceiling here is a fragment of a *manta*; this was a cloth hung just below the ceiling of dirt-roofed buildings to catch some of the more-or-less constant cascade of dust and fine dirt that settled through the old roofs as they weathered, expanded and contracted with changes in temperature, and settled. Cleaning or replacing the *manta* was a yearly spring-cleaning ritual.

PAGE 130. *Lower San Francisco Plaza, 1976.*

   A vine, unperturbed by the slight difference between adobe and the soil its roots are in, has climbed through a thick wall and into the church.

PAGE 131. *San Miguel, La Puente, 1975.*

PAGE 132. *Rear of the Church, Medanales, 1987.*

PAGE 133. *Santo: San Antonio, 1976.*

PAGE 134. *Oratorio, Tomé, 1974.*

PAGE 138. *Confessional, Maes, c. 1976.*

PAGE 139. *Pews, San Ignacio, c. 1976.*

PAGE 140. *Baptismal Font and Catafalque, Las Trampas, 1974.*

PAGE 141. *Sagrada Corazon in Lace, Placitas, 1986.*

PAGE 142. *Kneeler, Tomé, 1974.*

PAGE 143. *Confessional Doors, Villanueva, 1975.*

PAGE 144. *Interior, Aurora, 1975.*

BACK COVER: *Church Front, Ojitos Frios, 1987.*

SUGGESTED READING

Boyd, E. *New Mexico Santos: How to Name Them.* Santa Fe: Museum of New Mexico, International Folk Art Foundation, 1966.

Boyd, E. *Popular Arts of Spanish New Mexico.* Santa Fe: Museum of New Mexico Press, 1974.

Cordova, Lorenzo de [Lorin W. Brown]. *Echoes of the Flute.* Santa Fe: Ancient City Press, 1972.

Dickey, Roland. *New Mexico Village Arts.* Albuquerque: University of New Mexico Press, 1949.

Espinosa, José Edmundo. *Saints in the Valleys: Christian Sacred Images in the History, Life and Folk Art of Spanish New Mexico.* Albuquerque: University of New Mexico, 1967.

Jenkins, M.E. and A.H. Schroeder. *A Brief History of New Mexico.* Albuquerque: University of New Mexico Press, 1974.

Kessell, John L. *The Missions of New Mexico since 1776.* Albuquerque: Pub. for New Mexico Cultural Properties Review Committee [by] University of New Mexico Press, 1980.

Kubler, George. *The Religious Architecture of New Mexico.* Albuquerque: Pub. for School of American Research [by] University of New Mexico Press, 1974.

Pearce, T.M. *New Mexico Place Names: A Geographical Dictionary.* Albuquerque: University of New Mexico Press, 1965.

Warren, Nancy, *Villages of Hispanic New Mexico.* Santa Fe: School of American Research, 1989.

Williams, J., ed. *New Mexico in Maps.* Albuquerque: University of New Mexico Press, 1986.